www. wfg.woodwind.org

Handbook for Creative
Church Musicians

A Practical Guide to Composition and
Arranging by Harold Owen

GIA Publications, Inc.
Chicago

Publisher's Note

GIA Publications is most interested in encouraging creativity among church musicians. A lively pursuit of composition and arranging is essential as the church's needs change and grow. So is the development of compositional craft, which is necessary if creative talent is to be nurtured. To that end, we are pleased to offer this handbook. Professor Harold Owens is a much-respected teacher and author of composition and music theory, as well as a practicing church musician. It is hoped that this volume will serve as a practical, accessible resource—to guide and shape the creative offerings which are brought to the church.

Owen, Harold, 1931-
Handbook for Creative Church Musicians
ISBN 1-5799-115-7

CONTENTS

Preface

Is this book for me?

This is a book for those church musicians who wish to create special music for their choirs, organists, and congregations. Although some may have had extensive training and guidance in composition and arranging, others may have the desire to learn the skills necessary to create sacred music especially for the musicians under their charge. Still others may be church organists mainly interested in adding a creative facet to their function in the worship service.

This volume provides an abundance of practical information on many aspects of creating music for worship, and you will also find a strong dose of the fundamentals of voice leading, doubling, spacing, scoring, and other principles of basic harmony and counterpoint.

In the course of reading this book, if unfamiliar terms are encountered, please refer to the Glossary at the back of this volume. In addition, there are several appendices where many of the principles outlined in this book are presented in summary form.

What about computers and publication?

This book also contains some important information about the use of computers and music software for producing compositions, including scores and parts. The examples in this book have been formatted in *Finale*, one of the foremost music notation applications. Much information regarding use of *Finale* can be readily translated for use with other music notation programs. This book offers helpful tips on notation and score layout.

A chapter on preparing music to submit for publication is included. Publishers appreciate properly formatted and edited scores; a poor presentation may result in rejection, even though there is merit in the music itself.

Is this book for composers, arrangers, or people like me who have never before tried to create music for my church?

There is no substitute for compositional talent. The most skillful arranger may not have the capability to create an original anthem or organ work. However, the most talented composer who lacks the requisite skills in scoring, counterpoint, and harmony may not be able to produce works that can be performed by the available musicians or comprehended by the hearers. This book should help beginners to discover their talent and talented composers to gain the tools of the trade.

Some of the material presented here may seem quite basic and elementary, but upon careful examination, one is likely to find new information and some suggestions that can enhance creative efforts.

Who are you?

I am a composer and church musician. The principles discussed on these pages represent a life-long involvement as a teacher, conductor, and performer. For over thirty years, I have been teaching composition at a large state university, and during that time I have been the choirmaster of a fine local parish choir. The examples in this book were composed by me, unless otherwise indicated.

Since I am involved with a church that holds the liturgy in high esteem, my advice may be somewhat slanted toward the liturgical denominations—Roman Catholic, Episcopal, Lutheran, Greek Orthodox, and others. I have, however, tried to present information that would be applicable to church musicians of any denomination.

Harold Owen
Eugene, Oregon

Introduction

Music has been an integral part of worship throughout the history of humankind. Those who were responsible for music in the church not only performed it and trained others to perform it, they created it themselves. Josquin Desprez, Lasso, Palestrina, Byrd, Schütz, and J. S. Bach made their living as church musicians. They secured their positions due to their abilities as composers, not because they were charismatic conductors or facile organists.

What are some of the opportunities for me as a creative church musician?

It would be hard to find a position as Kapellmeister these days, a position which required the production of original music, yet some of today's most prominent church musicians are composers. A growing number of organists, choir directors, and ministers of music are trying their hand at creating music for wor-ship in their own churches. They are discovering many opportunities for creative expression. Some of these are relatively mechanical, others require elementary skills in arranging, and still others demand compositional skills and talent. Here are some of these opportunities, beginning with simpler ones and moving toward more demanding ones:

- transposing hymns, service music, or anthems to a more comfortable key for choirs and congregations

- composing introductions or interludes for use with hymns

- writing descants for singers or for instruments

- providing simple keyboard accompaniments

- making new harmonizations for hymns

- recasting a four-part anthem for two or three parts

- composing a short organ prelude on a hymn or chant

- creating an anthem based on a hymn or chant

- setting psalms for congregational singing, for choir, or for responsive singing using a cantor

- setting service music or music for the liturgy—parts of the mass, canticles, graduals, responses, the call to worship, amen, alleluia, and so on

- creating original anthems

- creating original organ works

- composing large-scale sacred compositions such as cantatas, masses, requiems, or oratorios

We hope that this book will help you with many of these tasks. When it comes to larger works, you should seek guidance from a reputable composer through private study or college-level course work and studio instruction.

What should I consider before submitting my work for publication?

Hundreds of thousands of short pieces of sacred music are being created each year, and many of these are reviewed by publishers. It is a sad fact, however, that many of these pieces are flawed by a lack of good voice leading, harmonization, contrapuntal skill, and scoring techniques. In the following chapters, you will find many good technical tips, but you will also find a reiteration of the basic principles of good harmony, counterpoint, and scoring. In addition, we will offer advice on the use of the computer, a marvelous tool that can save hours of work and produce beautiful, error-free scores.

Perhaps the best advice you will get from this book is to get help from arrangers and composers to review your music before you submit it for publication. In addition, there are courses in elementary composition and arranging available at local community colleges and courses offered through university extension.

Are there other ways I can enhance the quality of worship through music?

The choir director, organist, and minister of music have many opportunities for education—of the choir, of the clergy, and of the congregation. You are the expert on sacred music. Your church community should look to you for the best choice of music for all occasions, and some of it may be music you create. In your rehearsals with a choir, you should take every opportunity to educate your singers on the need for a variety of expression from the great sacred heritage of the past as well as the excitement, challenge, and potential appropriateness of new music—especially music you create for your own musicians.

There can be opportunities for you to give lectures, Lenten courses, a music sermon, or a concert dedicated more to enlightenment than to performance or entertainment. The congregation will thank you for making a few comments about a new work you will perform, especially if you created it.

If you are to be effective in your role as an educator, you should avail yourself of the history of sacred music and the great liturgies, of hymnody, of the role of music in your denomination and your own church or parish.

I've never tried writing music before. Where shall I start?

Choose a familiar hymn such as "Joy to the World." Write a simple harmony part for it. Sing through this new part and try adding some decorative pitches (passing tones or other chord tones). Make the part as singable as possible. Try moving the notes of the part in the opposite direction to some of the tones of the melody. Change the rhythm of the part so that it doesn't always have the same rhythm as the melody's rhythm. Let your melody have some movement during the longest notes of the hymn. It is even possible to let this "countermelody" cross over the hymn tune when it moves to lower pitches. Ask if this new musical line makes sense as a melody all by itself? What you have written is a descant that can be played or sung (if given the text). Chapter 1 is all about descants and provides some examples.

About the Author

HAROLD OWEN was born on December 13, 1931 in Los Angeles. He is Professor Emeritus of composition, musicianship, and music history; and former chairman of the department of composition at the University of Oregon School of Music. In addition he has been the director of the University Collegium Musicum and the University Consort, a faculty ensemble devoted to the performance of early music.

He received the B.Mus. degree in 1955 and the M.Mus. degree in 1957 from the University of Southern California, both with honors. After teaching in the public schools of Hopland, California from 1957 to 1959, he served as Composer-in-residence in Wichita, Kansas under the Contemporary Music Project sponsored by the Music Educators National Conference from 1959-60.

Owen returned in 1960 for doctoral study at the University of Southern California on a scholarship from Broadcast Music, Inc., served as a Graduate Teaching Fellow the following year, then joined the USC faculty in 1962 to teach theory and composition until 1966. He completed the DMA in composition at USC in 1972.

He became a member of the John Biggs Consort during the early 1960's and toured with the group during summers. This association led to his establishment of the University Consort shortly after joining the faculty of the University of Oregon School of Music in 1966. The Consort has performed regularly throughout the Northwest since then. He has remained on the faculty of the University of Oregon School of Music to the present, where he is teaching part-time post retirement.

Harold Owen has written a large number of compositions for chorus, orchestra, wind ensemble, and a variety of solos and chamber ensembles, both vocal and instrumental. Many of his choral works are in print as well as works for organ and various chamber ensembles. He has won several composition awards and commissions as well.

Owen's textbook *Modal and Tonal Counterpoint, Josquin to Stravinsky* was published in 1992 by Schirmer Books, New York. The book, now in its seventh printing, has been used widely in America and abroad. He has developed and updated a set of course materials for tutorials in the use of *Finale*, an excellent computer music notation application. The set of tutorials, updated recently for the current version of *Finale*, are available on the Internet and have been used by many individuals and schools around the world (including translations into Russian, Norwegian, and Portugese). His text, *Music Theory Resource Book,* was published in 2000 by Oxford University Press. His most recent project is a book of exercises in first-year composition, and it is being considered for publication by Oxford as well.

He continues to be active as composer, teacher, and adjudicator. He is currently teaching two of the three terms of his acclaimed course in counterpoint at the University of Oregon.

Prof. Owen has been choirmaster at St. Mary's Episcopal Parish, Eugene, Oregon for more than twenty years, where he established the Philharmonia Sacra Concerts devoted to the performance of liturgical music. He has written a large number of works for the church, many of which have been published, including anthems, organ works, two books of trumpet descants to familiar hymns, and a collection of hymn harmonizations published by G.I.A. Publications, Chicago.

Besides composing and conducting, he is a performer on piano, harpsichord, recorders and other renaissance wind instruments. His favorite outdoor activities are hiking and cross-country skiing.

CHAPTER 1. Descants

Nothing enlivens a hymn quite like a descant. Festive occasions such as Easter, Pentecost, and Christmas are enhanced by the bright sound of trumpet descants. Your sopranos will welcome the chance to make a special contribution above a familiar tune, and the congregation gets a lift from singing the melody and hearing the joyous counterpoint.

Writing descants is a good way for a church musician to take that first plunge into creativity—far less challenging than other tasks such as reharmonizing hymns, rearranging choral pieces, or composing new works.

Instrumental Descants

Take a critical look at this descant for the tune ST. GEORGE'S WINDSOR, the familiar Thanksgiving hymn "Come, Ye Thankful People, Come," then consider the questions that follow.

Ex. 1-1 Descant on ST. GEORGE'S WINDSOR.

1. *Why does the descant start with a rest?*
2. *How is the descant a good rhythmic foil for the hymn tune?*
3. *What motives unify the descant? How does it achieve variety? Is it a satisfying melody in its own right?*
4. *How are the sequences (melodic patterns) in the hymn tune reflected in the descant?*
5. *What intervals between the parts appear most often?*
6. *What accompanying harmonies do the descant and hymn tune project?*
7. *Which instruments would be able to play this descant? Of those, which would be most appropriate? Which would be least appropriate?*

If the descant and the hymn verse begin on the same beat, the instrumentalist would need to be cued by a conductor. Beginning with a rest not only assures good coordination, but it helps to create a contrapuntal distinction between hymn tune and descant. This distinction is heightened by the descant's eighth-note motion compared to the quarter-note motion in the hymn tune. Once again, remember that a good descant should be able to stand alone as a satisfying melody.

Any good composition must maintain a balance between unity and diversity. In the example, the leaps of a perfect fourth and the descending scale passages create unity. Variety can be seen in the rhythmic motion and the changes in melodic direction. Notice how the descant explores the off-beats, while the tune always moves on the strong beats. The descant tends to move during long notes in the tune.

This hymn tune is nicely crafted with repeated phrases and a number of sequences. Such a tune invites the composer of the descant to vary the melodic writing when there are repetitions and to use sequences where they occur in the tune (see measures 5 and 6, 13 and 14).

If you were to write down all of the intervals formed between the descant and the tune, you would soon realize that thirds and sixths appear most frequently, especially when notes occur at the same time. Melodic motion is most often *oblique,* one part moving while the other is at rest. *Contrary* motion is more frequent than *similar* or *parallel* motion, and the parts are never allowed to move in parallel fourths, fifths, seconds, or sevenths. Parallel motion almost always involves thirds or sixths, never unisons or octaves except for a phrase that doubles the hymn tune. These comments are nothing more than a brief statement of basic principles of counterpoint. You will find them more fully summarized in Appendices A and B.

Obviously, the descant must agree with the harmonies in the hymnal. The descant alone should project these harmonies. Chordal motion in the melodic writing helps to define the harmony. Although the descant may at times follow some pitch motion in the alto or tenor, it should avoid doubling the tune and the bass line. Below is the tune with chord symbols to indicate the accompanying harmony.

Ex. 1-2 ST. GEORGE'S WINDSOR with chord symbols

A number of instruments could play this descant. Among them are flute, oboe, clarinet, saxophone, recorder, trumpet, and violin. Of these, the best choices would be trumpet and oboe, or perhaps even saxophone. Flute descants must be placed in the upper part of the treble staff and above in order to be heard. Only the very highest octave of a recorder would penetrate through the voices and organ. Descants for horn or trombone can be very successful, but they must be quite independent of the rhythmic motion of the tune.

Before you begin to write a descant, be sure to determine the instrumentalist's capabilities and limitations. Most competent trumpeters, for example, can manage quite well with descants that stay within the range of (written) Middle C to High C, but care must be taken not to keep the tessitura (notes most often used) in the top fourth of this range. Note that in the example the descant occasionally crosses below the tune. The rests give the player plenty of opportunities for taking breaths. Fanfare-like writing is suitable for hymns of praise. Hymns of mystery, prayer, or supplication call for less active descants, but they can be very effective when played by flute or string instruments.

A good descant will agree in style with the hymn tune. Chorales should be given baroque-style descants, for example. Modal melodies may be used with modal tunes. Spirituals and hymns in "gospel style" can support descants containing "blue notes" (flatted third or seventh degrees of the scale).

Melodic imitation is especially attractive in a descant if the hymn tune will support it. Ex. 1-3 shows the beginning of an imitative descant to the tune GLORIA ("Angels We Have Heard on High.")

Ex. 1-3 Imitative descant.

Choral Descants

The principles for writing instrumental descants apply as well to choral descants, with the additional consideration of setting the text. Examine the following descant to the last verse of NEW BRITAIN ("Amazing Grace.")

Ex. 1-4 Choral descant for "Amazing Grace".

1. *Other than the text, how does a choral descant differ from an instrumental one?*
2. *How does this descant remain melodically independent from the hymn tune?*
3. *What is the range of the descant? How would you describe its tessitura?*

4. What elements in the descant create unity, and what elements create diversity?

Instrumental and choral descants share many characteristics. If a descant is sung or played alone, it should present a pleasing melodic shape, contain motives that unify it, have rhythmic variety, and yet be independent from the tune it accompanies. Choral descants tend to be less florid, smaller in range, and do not cross below the hymn tune as frequently as instrumental descants. In Ex. 1-4 the descant moves when the tune is stationary, and the melody is often in contrary motion to the tune. The range is a ninth, and the tessitura is relatively high. Although sopranos are usually given the descant to sing, a good effect can be achieved by allowing the tenors to double the sopra-nos on the descant.

The descant's text is generally set parallel with the text of the hymn tune. Some displacement of syllables, however, may be desirable (see Ex. 1-6). For tunes that have unusually long notes at the ends of phrases, such as "Jesus Walked This Lonesome Valley," the descant text can easily follow after the tune's text.

Ex. 1-5 The descant text follows the tune text.

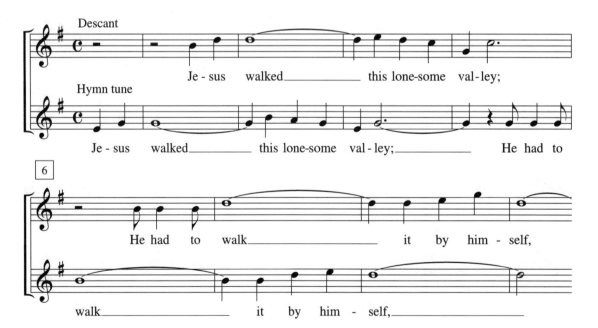

The descant in Ex. 1-6 is more melismatic (several notes sung on one syllable). Rests offer convenient places for the sopranos to breathe, and the offset syllables enhance the independence of the descant melody.

Ex. 1-6 Descant for DOWN AMPNEY ("Come Down O Love Divine").

A simple but effective descant can be created by giving the tenor part in the hymnal to the sopranos and the melody to all other parts. This is most successful when the tenor part is melodically interesting and lies somewhat higher than the melody when sung by sopranos. Ex. 1-7 shows a descant using the tenor part from Bach's setting of the chorale LIEBSTER JESU.

Ex. 1-7 Descant derived from the tenor part of LIEBSTER JESU.

In early metrical psalm settings, the tune was often set in the tenor. Hymnals in colonial America and later in the South perpetuated this tradition. In the singing schools that use shape-note hymnals such as *Southern Harmony*, both men and women would sing the tune and the uppermost part, resulting in a six-voice texture. Choirs should be encouraged to use the traditional settings of tunes from this repertoire, such as WONDROUS LOVE, and sing them in this manner.

Problems and Solutions

Ex. 1-8 shows a descant for the tune AURELIA ("The Church's One Foundation") that contains a number of common problems. Some are contrapuntal flaws and others are harmonic errors. Can you identify each of those problems marked?

Ex. 1-8 Descant with common flaws.

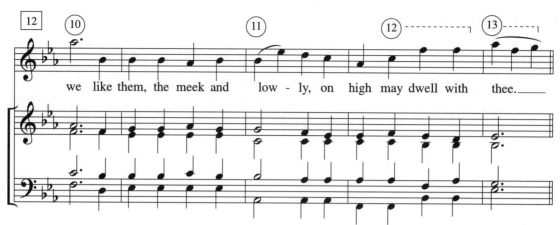

we like them, the meek and   low - ly, on high may dwell with   thee.____

This descant as a whole lacks rhythmic independence from the hymn tune except for the brief motion in measures 10 and 16. The contour of the descant melody follows too much the contour of the hymn melody, and it is not very attractive if sung by itself. Specific problems have been indicated by number.

1. Too much repetition of a single pitch makes for a dull melody.
2. The descant's pitch disagrees with the hymn's harmony.
3. Although parallel thirds with the melody usually give a good effect, these pitches move in parallel octaves with the bass.
4. When the descant is allowed to repeat the previous pitch as does the hymn tune, it makes a dissonance with the harmony.
5. The descant should not leap up when the hymn tune leaps up as well, especially when both parts come to a unison.
6. The tritone (augmented fourth or diminished fifth) is a difficult interval for most singers. Both pitches need to resolve by step (D to E♭, A♭ to G), but neither do.
7. This is an awkward pitch sequence. The A♭ wants to resolve to G, and the A♮ wants to resolve to B♭.
8. The leading tone, D, should resolve to E♭.
9. The descant moves in parallel fifths with the bass.
10. Much too high for the "ee" vowel. The "ah, " "oh," and "oo" vowels sound better in this register.
11. The harmony on beat one of measure 14 includes two appoggiaturas (an embellishing note, usually one step above the note it precedes), the melody note G and the tenor note B♭, both of which resolve downward in the hymn setting. The B♭ in the descant is a poor choice, especially since it leaps to the next pitch.
12. The descant moves in parallel fifths with the tune.
13. This figure has become a particularly tiresome cliché, it disagrees with the harmony, and it is too high for the vowel.

Ex. 1-9 Improved descant.

Yet_ she on earth hath un - ion with God, the Three in One,_____ and

mys - tic sweet com - mun - ion with those whose rest is won._____ O

hap - py ones and ho - ly Lord, give us grace that we____ like

them, the meek and low - ly,_ on_ high may dwell with thee.

The descant has been rewritten in Ex. 1-9 above. Some of the characteristics of this version are:

1. Melodic and rhythmic independence of the descant and hymn tune are maintained throughout. Melismas are used where there are long notes in the hymn tune.
2. This descant could be used as an instrumental or choral one. A positive feature is that dotted quarter–eighth rhythms will offset some weak syllables in the text when used as a choral descant.
3. Although there is some doubling of voice leading with the alto or tenor, care has been taken to avoid doubling in parallel fifths and octaves with the tune and the bass part.
4. The descant always agrees with the harmony of the hymn.
5. The vowel sounds "ee," "eh," "ih" (as in "with"), and "uh" (as in "the") should not be set on high pitches. In this text, the words "earth," "mystic," "rest," "we," "meek," and "thee" are kept out of the highest register. The word "us" in measure 11 might be considered a borderline case, but it lasts only a quarter note, and if the vowel is shaded toward "ah" somewhat, it will not be a problem.
6. Scalewise motives and broken chords unify the melody of the descant. Some new motives in the second half provide variety.
7. When the hymn tune moves to a higher tessitura, the descant is allowed to cross below it in order to avoid uncomfortably high notes.
8. Melodic motion is generally stepwise. Decorative pitches are passing tones and neighbor tones for the most part. Leaps are harmonic—movement between tones of the prevailing harmony.
9. The highest pitch is reached only once.

Sometimes a satisfactory descant can be derived from the tenor part, as in Ex. 1-7. The tenor part in this case, however, would make a very dull descant.

A good descant should call attention to itself because of its elegance, not because the sopranos (or an instrument) are simply performing something other than the hymn tune.

CHAPTER 2. Harmonization

One of the most common tasks for a creative church musician is providing a given melody with harmony. It may be as simple as a lead sheet for guitar accompaniment, or as challenging as providing an alternate harmonization for a hymn.

The Lead Sheet

For those unfamiliar with the term, a lead sheet is the notated melody with chord symbols to indicate the harmony. Many song books and some hymn books are presented in this manner. The accompaniment is improvised by guitar or piano (or even a small ensemble), using the chord symbols as a guide. Ex. 2-1 is a lead sheet for GREENSLEEVES (usually sung to the words "What Child is This?").

Ex. 2-1 Lead sheet for GREENSLEEVES.

1. *How and when would you use this lead sheet?*
2. *Would you use this setting for a guitar in addition to the organ for hymn singing?*
3. *What is the harmonic rhythm in the example?*
4. *How are chords chosen for a melody like this?*
5. *The tune* GREENSLEEVES *exists in a number of versions that differ from this one. Would the choice of chords be different in another version?*
6. *This example represents a very simple chordal setting. How would you change it to produce a more colorful setting?*
7. *All of the chords indicated are in root position. How do you indicate inversions? How can the symbols show that an inner voice is a suspension or an appoggiatura?*

This simple setting could be used for unison singing with guitar, piano, or autoharp as the accompaniment. It would work well with children's choir, singing outdoors, or in a camp setting. It is unsophisticated and leaves room for some improvisation. It is very unlikely that it would be used when the organ or piano is playing from a hymnal, which will have a much more complicated harmonization. Ex. 2-2 shows a lead sheet that uses the harmony found in a well-known hymnal.

Ex. 2-2 Lead sheet based on a hymnal harmonization.

The average rate of harmonic change per measure is called the *harmonic rhythm*. In Ex. 2-1 it is one per measure. At cadences it increases to two per bar, a common occurrence. In Ex. 2-2 the harmonic rhythm is generally one per bar, but some measures have two or three changes for the sake of variety.

Harmonic rhythm is a very important factor in good harmonizations, one that is often ignored by beginners. It should be stable, not erratic. Eighteenth-century chorales generally have a harmonic rhythm of four changes to the measure. Nineteenth-century hymns often have a slower harmonic rhythm. A poor effect would result if a piece were to begin with one harmony for four measures, changing to four harmonies in the next bar.

A strong melody will suggest suitable accompanying harmonies. The strongest pitches in the melody will be chord members, unless they are obviously appoggiaturas. The beginning pitches in Ex. 2-1 are E, G, A, B. The A is merely a passing tone, so the suggested harmony is E minor. In Ex. 2-2 with a quicker harmonic rhythm, the A is harmonized, becoming the fifth of a D major chord, and the G becomes the root of the next chord, G major.

When choosing harmonies for a melody, first decide on the prevailing harmonic rhythm. Ask yourself: "When do I sense the need for a new chord?" Once you have decided where a chord is needed, consider which chords contain the melodic pitch at that point. Some choices will seem obvious, others possible, and still others inappropriate. Consider also the effect that each chord you choose has on its neighbors. Using chords that belong to one key, the strongest progressions are chords whose roots are a fourth or fifth apart. Chords whose roots are a step apart result in a smooth progression. Chords whose roots are a third apart shift the harmonic color without making a strong progression.

It is a good practice to establish the key and mode at the beginning. The melody of GREENSLEEVES does quite a good job of establishing the Dorian Mode on E with the opening pitches (scale degrees 1-3-4-5-6-5). The following opening would go against the establishment of the key and mode:

Ex. 2-3 Poor harmonic choices for the beginning of GREENSLEEVES.

There are other problems here: The C chord should not continue across the bar where a chord change seems more appropriate. The C chord clashes with the C♯ in the melody (a cross relation). G followed by Am7 is a poor choice because the chords move in parallel with the melody. The last chord, Em, will make a full cadence where a half cadence is needed.

This tune dates from the sixteenth century, and it is most comfortable with harmonies suitable to Renaissance style. Although the chords chosen for Ex. 2-4 are exotic, they go against the style of the melody.

Ex. 2-4 Harmonies not suitable to the style of the tune.

Many of you may be more familiar with a version of GREENSLEEVES that uses a D♯ in measure 4, and still others are more used to a version in the Aeolian Mode, yielding C♮ in the first full bar. These differences would necessitate changes of some chords. Bar 4 would be accompanied by a B major chord. In bar 1, a chord with C♮ in it might be possible on the down beat.

Ex. 2-1 and 2-2 use standard harmonizations. It is possible to make a more colorful setting, provided you exercise good taste. A setting such as Ex. 2-5 has more harmonic changes and somewhat more colorful choices of chords. It could be used as the accompaniment for the final verse.

Ex. 2-5 More colorful setting of GREENSLEEVES.

Some points of interest in Ex. 2-5: the harmonic rhythm is very stable with two chords per bar; repetitions of phrases are given different harmonizations; some seventh chords are used to add color; several inversions are used; the final ending is allowed to have the *Picardy Third*—the E major chord. Note that when the lowest note is not the root of the chord, it is shown by a slash followed by the bass pitch. This is how inversions are indicated. A/C♯ indicates an A major chord in first inversion, with C♯ as the lowest tone. Am/E indicates an A minor chord in second inversion, with E as the lowest tone. The symbol "sus 4" in Ex. 2-2 indicates an appoggiatura on A that resolves to G in the next chord.

Chordal Keyboard Harmonization

Ex. 2-6 is a simple harmonization of PUER NOBIS by Michael Praetorius, which is usually sung to the words "That Easter Day with Joy was Bright." Study it, then consider the questions below.

Ex. 2-6 PUER NOBIS with simple chordal accompaniment.

1. *How would you describe the harmonic rhythm and texture of this setting?*
2. *How does the bass move compared to the melody?*
3. *The bass tones are chord roots most of the time. How do the other bass tones function in the chords?*

4. *How would you describe the cadences that occur every fourth measure? Which are the strongest cadences?*
5. *How does the root movement create variety in the setting?*
6. *What chord member is most often doubled? What other doublings do you find?*
7. *How does the voice-leading in this setting compare to voice-leading you would find in a four-part choral setting?*

A simple harmonization such as this would be used to accompany unison singing. The harmonic rhythm is generally one change per bar, and the texture is homophonic with chords in close spacing in the right hand with a somewhat independent bass line that is sometimes close to the right-hand chords and sometimes more than an octave below them.

The bass part

The bass line is the first part to consider when harmonizing a given melody. The bass line of Ex. 2-6 makes a good counterpoint to the melody: it maintains independence from the melody through the use of contrary melodic and rhythmic motion (one moves while the other is stationary). The cadences for each of the four phrases are authentic (V - I), plagal (IV - I), plagal, and authentic[*]. All of these cadences involve leaps in the bass. The strongest is the last, with a falling fifth. The first and second cadences involve a rising or falling fourth. The third cadence is not as strong as the others by virtue of the third leap in the bass and the fifth of the chord in the melody which links the last two phrases into a period.

It is obvious that the structure of the melody must be carefully considered before any harmonies are assigned to it. Choice of chords is basically the same as it is in creating a lead sheet. Strong progressions are used at cadence points. Smooth progressions are good for the middle of phrases. A mixture of root movement by step, third, fourth and fifth can create harmonic variety.

Doubling

The root is doubled in most of the chords. In a few the fifth is doubled. When the fifth is in the bass, it is usually doubled in the chord. The second inversion chord is very unstable and is most often used in a strong cadence leading to the dominant chord. Beginning composers often make the

---

[*] A brief explanation of the Roman numeral chord numbering system may be found in Appendix C on pp. 127-128.

mistake of harmonizing from the top down, and the fifth is left for the bass. The chord third is least often doubled. When it is, the two voices should proceed in contrary motion. In measures 3 and 11 the bass moves up while the melody moves down. The leading tone and the seventh of a chord should not be doubled. A useful rule of thumb is "beware of doubling any notes that have an acciden-tal attached."

Voice-Leading

You may remember these suggested guidelines from your harmony class: When moving from one harmony to the next a) move each voice by step if possible (except in the bass), b) retain common tones, c) resolve the leading tone up by step, d) resolve the seventh down, e) don't move all voices in the same direc-tion, f) avoid parallel unisons, fifths, and octaves. Believe it or not, these are still valuable tenets. Some styles, however, will ignore some of these details. Debussy showed us that a good effect can be achieved by moving all voices together. It is called *chord planing* and can be useful for harmonizing folk-like melodies and jazz or popular-style melodies. It would be inappropriate for most hymn settings, however.

In our example, however, the chords in the right hand are not treated the same way as voice parts are in a four-part choral setting with respect to voice-leading. As long as the melody and chords move in opposition to the bass part, there should be no problem with parallel fifths or octaves.

Figured Accompaniment

Keyboard arrangements such as Ex. 2-7 and 2-8 are useful for accompanying solo voices or unison singing by the treble or adult choir. Simple figures work well when the keyboard includes the melody. When the melody is not doubled in the keyboard part, more elaborate figures can be used.

Ex. 2-7 A setting of LAND OF REST with figured accompaniment.

1. *How would you go about writing this kind of setting?*
2. *This type of texture requires what considerations for spacing, doubling, and voice-leading?*
3. *Will this arrangement be suitable for either piano or organ?*

A logical order of events for writing this kind of setting would be as follows: 1) Notate the melody. 2) Analyze the structure of the melody and decide on the location and type of cadences needed. 3) Choose the harmonies you wish to use, keeping in mind the appropriate harmonic rhythm. 4) Write out the bass line, making sure that it is a good counterpoint to the melody. 5) Decide on the characteristics of the pattern for the middle voice. Apply the pattern (allowing for some variation) to the harmonies you have chosen. 6) Play through the completed draft and make any small changes that will improve the arrangement.

Spacing in a three-voice texture like this is less critical than textures with four voices. The middle voice can be played by either hand when piano accompaniment is intended. The more quickly-moving part sounds best if it is close to the melody, however. Doubling is also less critical than with four voices, but with just three, you should try to have complete triads as much as possible. Broken-chord figures allow you to "assemble" harmonies richer than simple triads. Notice the F7 (V7 of IV inverted) at the end of bar 13 and the B♭6 in bar 15. A pianist playing this arrangement is likely to use the sustaining pedal. An organist can play a smoother legato with the melody and the middle part on the manuals and the bass on the pedals.

The setting below of ST. COLUMBA ("The King of Love") gives the keyboard part free rein by not doubling the tune. Here again, the bass part was composed first and made as smooth as possible, imitating the tune. The figure is designed to provide motion through beat two of the measure where the tune is always sustaining. The harmony is contained in the broken chord figures. Note that each member of the pattern makes smooth voice-leading to its counterpart in the next pattern. Since the tune is a traditional folk melody, some chord planing is used.

Ex. 2-8 Accompaniment for ST. COLUMBA does not double the melody.

Alternate Hymn Harmonization

A widespread practice exists in many churches for the
organist to play an alternate harmonization on a verse of a
hymn, usually the final verse. The effect can be quite spectacular
if the harmonization is a good one. The choir members need to
know when this will take place so that they will sing the tune in
unison.

Ex. 2-9, 2-10, and 2-11 show three different types of alternate harmonization. Christian Witt's hymn tune STUTTGART
is decorated by a short "cookie-cutter" pattern. The traditional
Hebrew melody YIGDAL (also known as LEONI) is accompanied
by chords that do not appear on the down beats. Joseph Parry's
tune ABERYSTWYTH is given an imitative treatment in all
parts.

Compare these examples, and consider the questions that
follow.

Ex. 2-9 Alternate harmonization for STUTTGART.

Ex. 2-10 Alternate harmonization for YIGDAL.

Ex. 2-11 Alternate harmonization for ABERYSTWYTH.

1. *How do these harmonizations get the attention of the congregation?*
2. *Which of these seems to be closest to the hymnal harmonies? Which seems to be the most different from the hymnal version?*
3. *What compositional devices give character to the setting of YIGDAL?*
4. *How is imitation treated in the setting of ABERYSTWYTH?*
5 *What styles are represented in these examples?*
6. *There is a modal cadence in Ex. 2-11. Where is it?*

When an alternate harmonization is played for the last verse of a hymn, it must get the attention of the hearers. The texture of Ex. 2-9 with its eighth note patterns will do the trick. The missing down beats and the rhythm of the accompaniment in Ex. 2-10 will catch everyone's attention. The imitative entries of all parts in Ex. 2-11 will certainly make themselves known. Other strategies which may be used are unexpected chords at the out-set, pedal point in the bass, and the use of chromatic harmony (see Ex. 2-12 and 2-13). It is well known that Charles Ives improvised hymn harmonizations at times, eliciting some negative comments from older parishioners.

The setting of STUTTGART ("Come, Thou Long-Expected Jesus" and other texts) is closest to the harmony found in most hymnals. The pattern of eighth notes in scalewise motion simply replaces longer notes found in the original hymnal version. The pattern appears in many of the parts other than the tune, sometimes in two at once in parallel thirds or tenths. The pat-tern can move up or down, and variations in it appear from time to time. Several of the preludes in Bach's *Orgelbüchlein* make use of this style of ornamentation.

The tune YIGDAL (or LEONI) is most often sung to "The God of Abraham Praise." In this setting the accompanying parts have their own chordal rhythm:

This rhythm creates an emphatic, joyous effect. To accommodate this effect, some of the original harmonies are delayed or changed. Some decorative harmonies are used in the last two bars for a grand ending. Another feature of this arrangement is the use of sequences, especially in the bass, that help to unify the setting.

Some hymn tunes will yield themselves to an imitative treatment. The tune ABERYSTWYTH is one of these. All parts are involved in the opening point of imitation. Each phrase of the melody is treated in the same imitative fashion. The two phrases in measures 9-10 and 11-12 are special because they create a sequence. The accompaniment engages in the sequence as well. The harmonies must suit the imitation, and consequently they depart more than the other examples from the hymnal version.

The style in these harmonizations is closer to baroque than any other. The modal cadence in Ex. 2-11, measure 8, gives some variety and fits the style of the melody. Ex. 2-12 and 2-13 demonstrate two very different styles.

Ex. 2-12 Excerpt from KING'S LYNN with alternate harmonization.

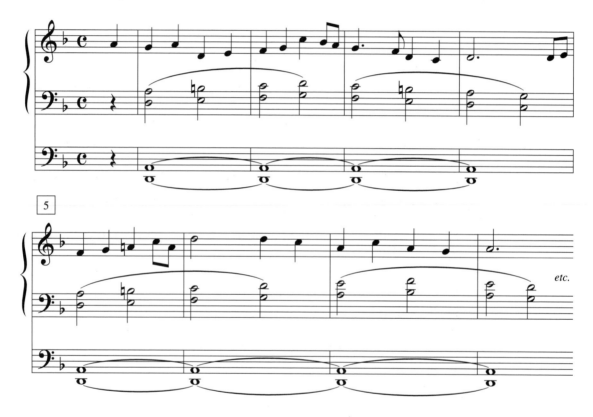

Ex. 2-13 Excerpt from NEW BRITAIN with alternate harmonization.

Virginia Harmony 1831, harm. by H. Owen

Ex. 2-12, KING'S LYNN, is an English folk melody that is modal. The pedal point and the left-hand part give a somewhat austere flavor to the setting which seems to suit the tune well. The fifths in the left hand would not be considered "parallel fifths" since they constitute a single part. Parallel fifths should be avoided between two parts that are intended to be in-dependent, not the case here.

The tune NEW BRITAIN ("Amazing Grace") has become intimately associated with gospel style. In Ex. 2-13, the meter gives a rocking feeling to the setting. The chromatic voice-leading and harmony are part of the gospel style as well.

Most congregations will welcome a broad variety of styles from medieval to modern, from classical to folk, even non-Western styles. The creative church musician has a chance to enhance and enliven worship through the judicious use of alternate hymn harmonizations.

CHAPTER 3. Arranging

Arranging may be as simple a process as writing out hymn parts for instruments, or as challenging as transforming an a cappella anthem for SATB into an anthem for SAB with keyboard accompaniment. A knowledge of instrumentation is necessary in the first case, and skills in harmony and counterpoint are needed for the second. There is not always music available for the particular musical resources which your situation has. Therefore, when some skill in arranging has been gained, the quality and quantity of music that can be brought to your church can be greatly expanded.

Instrumental Accompaniment for Hymns

1. *What kinds of ensembles can be used in the accompaniment for hymns?*
2. *Can the instrumentalists read their parts from the hymnal?*
3. *Which instruments are best suited for which parts?*
4. *Can recorders be used, or are they too soft to be heard?*
5. *What is the role of the organ when there is an instrumental ensemble playing?*
6. *How do I assign parts when the ensemble is larger than a quartet?*

On special occasions you may wish to invite an instrumental ensemble to accompany the hymns and other musical parts of the service. Some musicians may be able to play their part from the hymnal, especially violinists and cellists, but copyng out parts is a small task, especially using a computer and a good notation program. In addition, it is a sign of respect for the instrumentalists. If you have a string quartet, it is asking a lot of the violist to read the tenor part from a hymnal where it is given in the bass clef along with the bass. In any case, a photocopy of the hymns is the least you can do, since it is difficult to keep a hymnal open on a music stand.

Brass ensembles are most commonly used on festive occasions. A brass quartet will most likely consist of two trumpets with two trombones, trombone and tuba, or horn and trombone. Although many trumpeters own trumpets in C (good for high descants), you should expect to make parts for B♭

trumpets by transposing the part up a whole step (and changing to the appropriate key signature). Parts for horn are written a perfect fifth above the concert pitch. Trombones and tubas do not require transposed parts.

When hymnal parts are assigned, the soprano can be played by violins or oboes without transposition. Trumpets and B♭ clarinets require the transposition stated above. Flutes and recorders will sound better played an octave higher than written. The soprano recorder, like the piccolo, reads the soprano part as written but sounds an octave higher. The alto (or treble) recorder, when used in an ensemble, reads the same as the soprano. Solo music for alto recorder, however, is written and sounds *at pitch*. The tenor recorder's lowest pitch is actually middle C, so it can double only the soprano part. If you give it a tenor part, it will sound an octave higher. The bass recorder reads parts written in bass clef, but they sound an octave higher. Bass recorder can double either soprano or alto parts.

The alto part can be played by violin, viola, trumpet, clarinet, horn, bass recorder, and in a pinch, trombone. The tenor part can be played by viola, clarinet (except for notes that fall be-low third-line D in bass clef), horn, trombone, bassoon, cello, and guitar. Most guitarists are used to seeing their part written in treble clef, and the actual sound is an octave lower. If you give the tenor part to guitar, the part must be written an octave higher (like the tenor part in an open choral score). The modern choral tenor clef—treble with an 8 attached below—is becoming more commonly used for guitar parts.

The bass part can be played by cello, trombone, tuba, bassoon, bass clarinet, and guitar. Like the tenor saxophone, bass clarinet reads its part in treble clef transposed up a major ninth. If you assign the bass part to guitar, the player expects to see it written in treble clef (or in modern choral tenor clef).

Since all recorders play an octave above their instrument names, they sound well doubling hymn parts at the octave, especially when playing introductions or interludes. In every case, their low notes are very soft, and their highest notes are much louder. This is true of most wind instruments to a lesser or greater degree. It is just the opposite for the oboe and for saxophones, whose lowest notes tend to be the loudest.

Mixed ensembles pose special difficulties. Woodwinds (with the exception of saxophones and bassoon) can only match the dynamic level of brass instruments if they are pitched somewhat higher. Strings have difficulty matching brass instruments in intensity. Recorders and acoustic guitars cannot hope to compete with brass instruments. An ensemble of woodwinds and strings works well, and recorders and guitars can blend well if used with choir alone.

One of the most important considerations in the use of instrumental ensembles in a church setting is how the organ is to be used. For congregational hymn singing, a brass ensemble can be used without organ at all. The organ may join in on selected verses only. For lighter ensembles, the organ may be needed for congregational support. If the choir is to sing the hymn alone, the organ may not be necessary. A talented arranger may write independent parts for the organ and the ensemble. The organ may sometimes provide a modulating interlude before the last verse is sung in a higher key.

If the ensemble is larger than a quartet, you have the option of doubling parts or creating a new part. As was mentioned above, flutes and recorders are effective for doubling the melody an octave higher. Tuba and String Bass can double the bass line an octave lower. It is inadvisable to double the melody down an octave or the bass up an octave in most cases (an exception being the practice in singing shape-note hymns when some tenors double the sopranos and some sopranos double the tenors). Sometimes it is possible to double the alto or tenor parts an octave higher than written.

In creating arrangements, you need not have all of the instruments playing all of the time. For example, if there is a brass quintet (two trumpets, horn, trombone, tuba), the tuba may double the bass part down an octave in some of the phrases and rest during others. In the case of a woodwind quintet (flute, oboe, clarinet, horn, bassoon), the flute may play the melody at pitch some of the time and up an octave at other times. For a quiet verse, the oboe may be given the melody alone while the flute rests. For the sake of variety, you may wish to have the ensemble play the melody while the organ plays the other parts.

Adapting SATB to SAB

The chorale by Melchior Vulpius, Ex. 3-1, is often sung as an SATB anthem. Ex. 3-2 shows an SAB setting.

Ex. 3-1 GELOBT SEI GOTT setting for SATB.

Ex. 3-2 GELOBT SEI GOTT setting for SAB.

1. *In the SAB arrangement, what has been retained from the SATB version, and what has been changed?*
2. *In a choir with sopranos, altos, and a single part for the men, what is a good working range for the men's part?*
3. *What principles govern the choice of notes for the alto part?*
4. *Why are the altos allowed to sing higher than the sopranos in the last two bars?*
5. *What about keyboard accompaniment?*

The chorale tune is carried by the soprano and therefore was unchanged in the SAB setting. The bass part is mostly intact, but the lowest notes were moved up an octave in order to accommodate the men's voices, which will likely be a mixture of tenors and basses. A good working range for the "B" in SAB settings is first-space A to middle C or D. Obviously, the tenors will not be very effective below second-space C.

The original harmonies have been preserved as much as possible. The bass in measure 9, beat 3 has been changed to F so that the alto can have D. If the alto were to have F, there would be a tritone leap to B in the next bar. The inverted chord is in keeping with the early seventeenth-century style (the tune appeared in 1609).

With the outer parts virtually unchanged, it becomes the responsibility of the alto to represent both alto and tenor of the original. The alto pitches should complete the triads as often as possible. If the outer parts double the root, the alto should have the third. Seventh chords in three parts usually drop the fifth. The alto can create fuller harmony by moving through chord members. Examples of this are in measures 13 and 15 where the eighth-note motion completes the seventh chords. Disjunct motion within a chord can insure better voice leading. In measure 3 the alto and bass move to other chord tones to avoid parallel fifths that would otherwise result between beats one and three. The F♯ in measures 6 and 7 help prepare the cadence to G major. The completed alto part should be as melodically pleasing as possible. For that reason, the alto part in many SAB arrangements is somewhat more active than the other parts.

The tune dips very low at the end. The bass and soprano are both on C. An E is needed to complete the harmony, but E below middle C would be too low for the altos, which explains why the alto is allowed to move above the soprano for the ending. The lis-teners will still follow the tune in the soprano part.

There is a fine arrangement of this tune by Henry G. Ley to the text "The Strife is O'er." After a 4-bar introduction by the organ, the chorus sings the first verse in unison, the organ providing the harmony. A short organ interlude leads to the second verse set for men's voices in unison with the rest of the chorus adding harmony for the "alleluia." The third verse is in four-part harmony, unaccompanied, with the tune in the tenor, then the bass. At "alleluia," we find a soprano descant, the other voices in unison on the tune. The final verse gives the tune to the women's voices with organ providing the harmony, and the final "alleluia" is in harmony with the tune passed from tenor to alto to soprano. The piece ends with a short triumphal coda.

For our simple arrangement, the chorus could sing a cappella if it is capable, but keyboard support doubling the voices would also be acceptable. Since the harmonies have been preserved, the organ or piano could play the original.

The strategy for adapting hymns or anthems where the accompaniment does not simply double the voice parts is much the same as we have described above. Pitches left out of the original alto and tenor parts are covered by the keyboard part, so it is not so necessary to move the alto as much. Ex. 3-3 shows an excerpt from "Jesu, Joy of Man's Desiring" by Bach in a setting for three-part chorus.

Ex. 3-3 Excerpt from "Jesu, Joy of Man's Desiring" arranged for SAB voices.

The small notes in the example represent the original four-part choral setting. The pianist or organist can play them for discreet support of the voices and to complete Bach's original harmony. Arrangements such as this can bring some of the best of sacred music into the reach of smaller choirs.

In some pieces such as Mozart's "Ave Verum," the bass part of the accompaniment doubles the bass choral part, while the upper parts in the accompaniment are more independent from the voice parts. In such cases, the bass part may be omitted and all the men can sing the tenor part, with adjustment only when it is too high.

Variety in Hymn Singing

The time-honored way of singing hymns—the organ plays through the hymn and then the choir and congregation sing through all verses—is not the only way hymns may be sung Sunday after Sunday. There are many ways to vary hymn presentation. We have already discussed using alternate harmonizations. In this section we will examine some other ways to gain variety in hymn singing. Below is a sample of the order for singing a hymn as it might appear in the service folder.

Processional Hymn: VENI VENI EMMANUEL   **Hymnal No. 195**
Introduction: Solo recorder
Verse 1: Choir alone; the assembly joins in the refrain
    "Rejoice! Rejoice! Emmanuel shall come to thee, O Israel."
Verse 2: Choir and assembly in unison
Verse 3: All men in unison
Verse 4: Choir *a cappella*; the assembly joins at the refrain
Verse 5: All women in unison
Verse 6: Choir women with recorder descant
Interlude: Organ
Verse 7: All voices

---

1. *How will the hymnal be used by the congregation?*
2. *Assuming the melody begins on D above middle C, what type of recorder and what register would be effective?*
3. *When and how would you use the organ?*
4. *How will you score the parts for choir?*
5. *What could be the purpose of the interlude?*
6. *How might the scoring for Verse 7 be different from Verse 2?*

The strategy for singing the hymn given above would be rather elaborate for "ordinary time," but would be quite appropriate for a festive occasion, such as the First Sunday in Advent or a "Festival of Lessons and Carols." It shows several possibilities that could be used to vary hymn singing on ordinary Sundays. The hymnal provides the congregation with the complete tune* and all stanzas of the text. It would not be difficult for anyone to follow the instructions in the service

---

* The version of VENI VENI EMMANUEL used here follows the rhythm of the chant. Some hymnals have a metrical version that prolongs the final notes of each phrase.

leaflet, and it is convenient to have the text to follow for the parts sung only by the choir.

Instead of an organ introduction, the solo recorder, played from the back of the church, would be a lovely way to introduce this familiar modal hymn. The tune has a range of middle C to the C an octave higher. This is not a good range for soprano or tenor recorder because if it is played in the lower register, it is very weak, and if played in the higher register, it reaches difficult and shrill notes. Alto recorder would be the best choice; bass recorder would be possible as well. Alto would play an octave higher than written in the hymnal. A bass recorder would play at pitch. During the introduction, the choir is in procession.

It is likely that the choir would still be in procession for the beginning of the first verse, and unaccompanied unison singing would be appropriate. The assembly would then join in at the refrain, still without accompaniment.

Verse 2 is sung by all, in the usual way with organ playing the accompaniment that is written in the hymnal. For Verse 3 all men will sing in unison, the organ continuing with the hymnal accompaniment.

Since most hymnals give a unison setting for voices, the setting for the choir for Verse 4 gives you an opportunity to make an arrangement. Ex. 3-4 shows a sample beginning.

Ex. 3-4 The first two phrases of VENI VENI EMMANUEL for SATB.

With all women singing in Verse 5, there is an opportunity for the organ to play an alternate harmonization. Richard Proulx has written a fine alternate accompaniment that is lighter, suitable for women's voices. The first two phrases are quoted in Ex. 3-5.

Ex. 3-5 Alternate accompaniment for VENI VENI EMMANUEL by Richard Proulx, first two phrases.

Setting © 1975, GIA Publications, Inc.

Verse 6 will be the lightest verse. The choir sopranos sing softly, the organ plays softly, and the alto recorder can be heard easily, playing a descant like the one shown in Ex. 3-6.

Ex. 3-6 Recorder descant for VENI VENI EMMANUEL, first two phrases.

The organ interlude can be used for a modulation to a higher key. Ex. 3-7 shows a short interlude that prepares for the final verse to be sung in E minor.

Ex. 3-7 Interlude modulating to E minor.

The final verse, now in E minor, is sung by all, and it is another opportunity for a final grand harmonization, such as shown in Ex. 3-8.

Ex. 3-8 A new harmonization for the final verse of VENI VENI EMMANUEL.

CHAPTER 4. Chorale Preludes

Preludes and postludes give an organist the opportunity to offer something special to the worship service. Often, the music is based on hymns or chants appropriate for the season of the church year, especially in the denominations that observe the "liturgical year." The chorale prelude can be a good choice for your first attempts in original composition. The piece may be relatively short; the melody is given; and it carries with it a simple phrase structure with defined cadence points. The common harmonies for the melody can be used, decorated, or altered.

The *Cantus Firmus*

Below is a hymnal setting of the opening phrase of OLD HUNDREDTH.* Compare each of the settings with it, and consider the questions that follow.

Ex. 4-1 The first phrase of OLD HUNDREDTH with various settings.

---

* Some hymnals present this tune with all quarter notes or half notes.

1. *What is a cantus firmus? What is the distinction between organ prelude and chorale prelude?*
2. *Where does this familiar tune come from?*
3. *The hymnal setting represents what period of style?*

4. *What is the texture of Ex. 4-1b? How are the alto, tenor, and bass parts related to the hymnal version?*
5. *How would you describe the texture of Ex. 4-1c? How are the harmonies related to those in Ex. 4-1a?*
6. *Ex. 4-1d is a homophonic setting with the tune in the bass. How does this arrangement affect the harmonies?*
7. *How is the tune treated in Ex. 4-1e?*
8. *Ex. 4-1f is a canon at the octave. How has the melody been changed? How can this be used in a chorale prelude?*

The *cantus firmus* is literally the "fixed song," the given melody. It is sometimes referred to as the *cantus prius factus,* the "previously made song." Any melody may be used as a cantus firmus, but shorter, simpler, familiar melodies are best. Hymns, chorales, and chant melodies are by far the most commonly used today. For a time, during the Renaissance, even secular tunes were used for the cantus firmus.

The given tune used in a prelude is most often found in the topmost voice, but it can be found in other voices, especially the bass, and it may appear as a canon in two voices. It must be clearly identifiable from the other voices by the listener. In most cases it is set apart by having longer note values than the accompanying parts.

The term *organ prelude* can denote any music played on the organ before the service proper begins. However, a *chorale prelude* was originally a decorative setting of a Lutheran chorale for the organ. Today the term refers to an organ prelude based on a hymn tune, regardless of its origin or type. Bach has given us a superb collection of various types of chorale preludes in his *Orgelbüchlein,* that continue to serve as models for us today.

The tune, OLD HUNDREDTH was a melody originally used for Psalm 100. It comes from a French Psalter by the name of *Pseaumes octante trois de David,* 1551. The harmonization is by Louis Bourgeois (ca. 1510-ca. 1562) in the *Genevan Psalter,* which is mid-Renaissance. It is best known as the melody for the Doxology ("Praise God, from Whom All Blessings Flow"), but it is sung as a hymn to various texts, including "All People That on Earth Do Dwell," and "From All That Dwell below the Skies."

Ex. 4-1b is a polyphonic setting made by elaborating the original alto, tenor, and bass parts. A simple pattern or motive is applied to various parts in turn. This is the simplest, most straightforward type of chorale prelude.

Ex. 4-1c is a three-part layered texture with the tune on top, a running part in the middle, and a bass part that has its own rhythmic character.

Ex. 4-1d is homophonic, with the cantus firmus in the bass. This requires special treatment of the harmony, since many of the original triads will be inverted.

In Ex. 4-1e the opening phrase of the tune is used as a subject for a three-part fugue. The example includes a short exposition and the beginning of the development with a middle entry on C in the bass.

The tune has been altered rhythmically in Ex. 4-1f for use as a canon. In a chorale prelude the canon would occupy two parts with decorative counterpoint in the other parts.

Contrapuntal Elaboration

As mentioned above, the chorale prelude that is constructed by contrapuntal elaboration of the original four-part setting is the easiest to compose. Bach's setting of CHRIST LAG IN TODESBANDEN from *Orgelbüchlein* exemplifies this technique. The figure, consisting of a double neighbor group, is used to elaborate the alto, tenor, and bass of the chorale setting. In Ex. 4-2 the chorale harmonization is given above the chorale prelude.

Ex. 4-2 CHRIST LAG IN TODESBANDEN from *Orgelbüchlein* by J. S. Bach.

The double neighbor figure fits nicely where the chorale harmonization has descending eighth notes. Once the figure has been established, it can be varied in a number of ways such as the passing tone and escape tone in the tenor in measure 1, beat 4, or the two upper neighbor tones in the alto in measure 2, beats 1 and 2. The figure is distributed equally between alto and tenor. Because of its role as the harmonic bass, the pedal part has fewer of these figures. At cadence points there are always eighth notes, establishing each new tonic area with scale degrees 4-5-1. Note that the motion in the lower parts does not stop with the last note of each phrase of the tune, thereby creating a seamless flow throughout. Try the short exercise in Ex. 4-3.

Ex. 4-3 Exercise: Complete the embellished version of the second phrase of OLD HUNDREDTH below, using Ex. 4-1b as a guide.

Decide first where the figure will go next. Make sure that the second eighth note does not create improper parallels with any of the other voices. The figure can be varied as you can see in Ex. 4-1b: beginning with a rest or a note, moving up or down from the second eighth note, moving scalewise. If there is a leap from the second eighth, that note must either be consonant in the chord or be an escape tone (as in the alto part, Ex. 4-1b).

When two parts are embellished at the same time, make sure that they make consonances (thirds and sixths) with each other. Try to move the bass part in contrary motion to the soprano whenever possible. If you were to string together the first phrase with the completed second phrase, you would need to add motion to the last bar of Ex. 4-1b.

Observe the proper spacing of parts: The distance between soprano and alto and between alto and tenor should not exceed an octave. The distance between tenor and bass is not limited.

English composers of the Elizabethan Era were very proficient in ornamenting the parts of a simple theme to create keyboard variations. Their name for the technique is "making divisions." Any part may have divisions, which can move from part to part. One way these composers insured that the voice-leading was maintained was to begin and end the divisions with the same pitch. This procedure can be very helpful in writing chorale preludes of the embellished harmony type.

The harmony itself can be embellished as well as the voice parts. A shift to another position (or inversion) of the harmony is a common practice (see Ex. 4-2, meas. 2, beat 1, and meas. 4, beat 1). The simple V-I cadence can be changed to IV-V-I or ii-V-I (meas. 6, beats 2 to 3). Secondary (or applied) dominant or diminished seventh chords can add color (see meas. 7, beats 3 and 4). Some of the notes of the melody can be given alternate harmonies (see meas. 10). When the chorale is in the minor, the third may be raised in the final chord.

Layered Texture

Bach's setting of DER TAG DER IST SO FREUDENREICH is an excellent example of a chorale prelude in layered texture. The first two phrases are shown in Ex. 4-4. The chorale harmonization has been rhythmically altered in order for you to com-pare more easily its harmonies with those of the prelude.

Ex. 4-4 DER TAG DER IST SO FREUDENREICH from *Orgelbüchlein* by J. S. Bach, the first two phrases.

This type of chorale prelude is characterized by the cantus firmus appearing in long notes in the uppermost part, one or more decorative parts in the middle, and a contrasting bass line that has slower motion than the inner part or parts. In this example, the alto and tenor create a single unit that completes and elaborates the harmony. A rhythmic pattern is established in the opening measure and developed continuously throughout the prelude.

The only real difference between the layered type of chorale prelude and the contrapuntal elaboration type is the independent character of the bass part that develops its own rhythmic and melodic patterns. Decoration of individual parts involves the same choices: passing tones, neighbor tones, escape tones, suspensions, appoggiaturas, double neighbor groups, and anticipations, as well as movement among chord tones. Elaboration of the harmony is the same as well for both types.

If there are only three parts, as in Ex. 4-1c, the active middle part will often touch on more than one chord tone before the next chord change. Broken chord figures and compound melody are good ways to provide fuller harmony. Spacing principles for three parts differ from those for four parts in that the distance between adjacent parts can exceed an octave. The middle part often occupies a larger range than either the alto or tenor in four-part music. It is inadvisable to allow close voicing below second space C in the bass clef.

Ex. 4-5 is a similar exercise using the Doxology tune, this time continuing with the second phrase from the end of Ex. 4-1c.

Ex. 4-5 Exercise: Complete the layered version of the second phrase of OLD HUNDREDTH below, using Ex. 4-1c as a guide.

Complete the bass part first, continuing its pattern. Sketch in the pitches needed in the middle part to complete the harmonies, then string them together with eighth notes. Try to use motives that appear in Ex. 4-1c. Play through the middle part alone to see that it makes a satisfactory melody—one where no pitches are overused, the shape is pleasant, and the chords formed with the soprano and the bass are complete. Play the bass part alone with the same things in mind. Check to see that you have not made a leap to the fifth of a triad when the harmony is changing.

Textures with the Melody in the Bass

If you set the melody of a hymn or chorale in the bass but still use the hymnal harmonization, a number of improper inversions may result. Compare the harmonization of LOBE DEN HERREN ("Praise to the Lord") taken from a hymnal, Ex. 4-6 with that of a simple three-part chorale prelude setting with the tune in the pedals, Ex. 4-7.

Ex. 4-6 LOBE DEN HERREN, hymnal version.

Ex. 4-7 Chorale prelude on LOBE DEN HERREN by the Author.

The first and last phrases of the tune end with the pitches *re - do.* The hymnal version sets this with the progression ii$_5^6$ - V - I. When these notes are in the bass, the cadence becomes vii°⁶ - I. The cadence in Ex. 4-7, measure 14 is to G Minor. If a half cadence were used there, as in the hymnal version, the G would produce an unsatisfactory V_4^6 chord.

The upper parts are in free imitation, developing a simple pattern. When Bach uses this texture, the upper parts are often in canon. A fine example of this is the first of his canonic variations on VOM HIMMEL HOCH. In some of his chorale preludes, Bach sets the chorale melody in the tenor, played on the pedals with a 4 ft. stop; the bass is played by the left hand.

As an exercise, continue Ex. 4-1d with the second phrase of OLD HUNDREDTH. The A that ends the phrase should not be harmonized with a D Major chord since it will be a V_4^6 . Some possibilities are ii, vii°6, and V of V.

Fugal Treatment

A chorale prelude can take the form of a *fugato,* or short fugue. In this type of prelude, the first phrase of the chorale is used as the fugue subject. Ex. 4-1e shows the opening of this type of fugue. You should not attempt this type of chorale prelude unless you are skilled in counterpoint.

In the *chorale motet* the first phrase of the chorale melody is introduced by fugal imitation before being stated in longer note values in the soprano. Each phrase of the chorale is treated in this manner. Ex. 4-8 shows how the chorale is presented in profuse imitation before appearing in the top part.

Ex. 4-8 GOTT UND HERR by J. S. Bach (BWV 693), first section.

Canonic Treatment

Composers for organ during the Baroque Era delighted in using canon in chorale preludes. There are more than a half dozen such pieces in Bach's *Orgelbüchlein* alone. The canon often involves the chorale itself, but other parts may be involved in canon as well. Because the chorales were not written with the idea of canon in mind, they usually need some alteration in order for them to be used in a canon. Ex. 4-1f demonstrates how OLD HUNDREDTH can be altered to form a canon.

In ERSCHIENEN IST DER HERRLICHE TAG, Ex. 4-9, Bach gives the chorale in canon to the soprano and bass. The inner parts complete the harmony with a short motive in parallel thirds or sixths.

Ex. 4-9 ERSCHIENEN IST DER HERRLICHE TAG,
    from *Orgelbüchlein* by J. S. Bach, first phrase.

Bach sets both the chorale and the accompanying voices in canon for IN DULCI JUBILO, Ex. 4-10. In this case, the pedal part responds to the chorale an octave lower as the tenor part. The bass part responds to the alto an octave lower. Note that the pedal part should be played on a 4′ stop, which sounds an octave higher than written.

Ex. 4-10 IN DULCI JUBILO from *Orgelbüchlein* by J. S. Bach, first phrase.

Ex. 4-11 presents an exercise in double canon. The two leading voices are given. Your task is to fill in the followers. The cantus firmus is the famous canon by Thomas Tallis.

Ex. 4-11 TALLIS' CANON: Complete as a double canon.

CHAPTER 5. Composing for Voices

The foregoing chapters dealt with creating music based on previously written melodies such as hymns and chorales. Writing completely original music calls for still more talent and skill.

Writing Melodies

The melodies below demonstrate a number of principles of melodic writing. The questions that follow should help to focus your attention on several of them.

Ex. 5-1 "Spirit of Power and Love".

Ex. 5-2 "They Cast Their Nets".

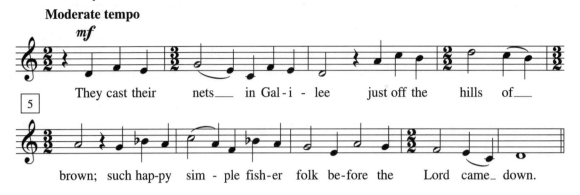

Ex. 5-3 "Arise, My Love".

Ex. 5-4 "This is the Day".

1. *What contours do you find in the phrases of these melodies?*
2. *Where are the climax points? How is a sense of direction created in each melody?*
3. *Some notes are obviously more important than others. What factors make these notes stand out?*
4. *What are the harmonic implications in these melodies? Can you get a sense of a suitable harmonic rhythm for each melody?*
5. *How would you describe the range and tessitura of each example?*
6. *Which pitches seem to require movement? Which pitches give a feeling of repose or resolution?*
7. *What is the difference in effect upon the listener between steps and leaps? What effect is created by two or more leaps in the same direction? What intervals are hardest to sing? How do we expect a melody to move after a large leap? How is style affected by the handling of leaps?*
8. *What elements in each melody provide a sense of unity? of variety?*
9. *How does the rhythm propel each melody forward?*
10. *How have the important words of the lyrics been given musical stresses?*

Melodic contour

By far the most common melodic shape is the arch. Several of the phrases in Ex. 5-1 through 5-4 have this shape. The first and second phrases of "Spirit of Power and Love" are shaped like arches. The last phrase of "This is the Day" is an arch with a small turn at the end. A phrase that rises in pitch from beginning to end is perhaps less common. The phrase beginning at measure 8, Ex. 5-1 moves up from E♭ to D♭ to prepare for the climax. Phrases that move downward are in Ex. 5-1, the phrase beginning in measure 22, and in Ex. 5-4, the opening phrase. Some phrases are wave-like, as can be seen in Ex. 5-2 and 5-3.

A melody that stays within a very limited range over an extended time is less desirable, unless it has very distinctive rhythmic motives or the accompanying parts give it changing harmonic color. Melodies that are mostly in one tessitura, then inexplicably shift to a different tessitura have a less appealing shape, as do melodies that reach their high or low points more than once. An exception to this is a melody whose highest or lowest pitch is treated as a reference tone, creating the effect of a pedal point (see Ex. 5-9).

Climax

The climax in a phrase is often reached at its highest point. Other factors can influence the climax, however, including dynamic level, rhythmic emphasis, the goal of a sequence, an extended melisma, or the point where the most important word in the lyric lies.

The climax usually takes a little time to build. If it occurs too early in the phrase, the rest of the phrase will seem anticlimactic. If there are two climactic points in a melody, they should not be of equal strength. The hymn "Joy to the World" set to its familiar tune ANTIOCH would seem to start with the climax, but the return up the scale to "King" is the real climax and serves as a pitch reference to the word "Joy."

The climax in "Spirit of Power and Love" occurs at its highest point in measure 14. It is also the highest dynamic level in the melody. The climax in "They Cast Their Nets" is less obvious. It occurs near the end on the words "fisher folk" following a sequence and introducing a new rhythmic motive, the *hemiola*. In "Arise, My Love," the climax builds in the pitch repetitions beginning in measure 11 until the F♯ alters the repetition on the words "the rain." The melisma on the word "rejoice" in bar 5 of Ex. 5-4 marks the climax which has been building through the repetition of the word and the rising pitch contour.

Important pitches

Some melodic pitches are more important structurally than others. As a composer, you will want to give some pitches more stress than others. Notes may stand out if they are:

1. longer, rather than shorter
2. higher, rather than lower
3. the first note or last note
4. on strong rather than weak beats
5. repeated
6. reached by large leap
7. followed by large leap
8. louder or accented, rather than softer
9. syncopated
10. following a rest
11. given stressed syllables of the text
12. appoggiaturas

Frequently the composer creates a succession of stressed pitches moving by step that carries the melodic line to its logical goal. Such a succession is called a "step progression." Several occur in "This is the Day." The step progressions are indicated in Ex. 5-5.

Ex. 5-5 Step progressions in "This is the Day".

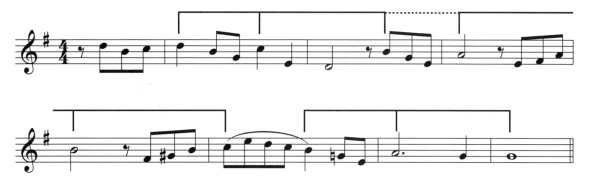

Strong cadences are important goals of melodic motion. The pitch that ends the phrase should not be preempted by appearing in a strong position just before the cadence. Note how fresh the C♮ sounds in measure 10 in "Arise, My Love." It would have been a mistake to allow that note to appear in bar 9.

Harmonic implications

Melodies that are mostly stepwise, such as "Spirit of Power and Love," will support a variety of harmonic settings. Those that contain leaps and triadic motion, such as "This is the Day," have more explicit harmonic implications. The melody is obviously in G Major. In measure 1 (remember that a pick-up bar is not considered the first measure) the harmonies are likely to be I and IV. The D in bar 2, will take I, iii, or V chords with equal success. The G♯ in bar 4 suggests a V of ii. For both of these melodies a harmonic rhythm of one or two to the bar is appropriate.

The melody of "They Cast Their Nets" is modal, and its harmonic progressions and cadences should be modal. Bar 2 could be harmonized by Am7 (or C) moving to Dm in bar 3. The final cadence might be B♭ - C - Dm. Harmonic rhythm seems to be one per bar until bars 7 and 8, where it changes to two.

There are frequent shifts of tonal focus in "Arise, My Love," and consequently harmonies are not predictable. In the anthem from which this melody is taken, the organ plays a sustained complex chord while a flute or oboe imitates the voice part a major sixth higher.

The important point is that the composer must be aware of the implied harmonies and harmonic rhythm of the melody as it unfolds. Failure to do so invites problems in scoring the accompanying parts.

Range and tessitura

The range of the melody in choral music is generally restricted to about a tenth, and the tessitura does not shift radically. Some of the best-loved melodies have a compass of an octave or less. Solo vocal music, on the other hand, may exploit the singer's ability and vocal quality, extending the limitations of range and tessitura. It is essential for the composer to ask for which voices or groups the music is intended—a solo, one section of the choir, high voices, or unison singing.

You can expect all sections of the average volunteer church choir to be limited in range. The voice ranges given below may seem very conservative to you, but if you restrict yourself to them, your music will be accessible to many more choirs than just your own local choir. Many of the greatest masterpieces of choral music adhere to these limits. Your basses may claim to be able to reach down to D below the staff, but the sound is weak and unsupported. Your sopranos may be able to reach High C, but when they do, you will wish you had not given them the chance. Tenors are ineffective below their staff, and altos fear to tread into the upper reaches of the treble clef unless they are doubled by the sopranos. In the chart, the open note heads show the range limits for most of the music. The filled note heads are pitches that should be used only occasionally.

Ex. 5-6 Voice ranges for the average volunteer church choir.

The ranges may be slightly extended when they are doubled. When doubled with tenors, the basses may reach E in louder passages. In softer ones, the tenors may sing with the basses down to a B♭. Altos may manage a few Es when doubling sopranos, and the sopranos may join the altos for a low B♭ in soft passages.

Ex. 5-1 was written for treble boys' voices. The range is a ninth, and the tessitura is moderate for trebles. The anthem can be sung by adult voices, however, for sopranos, tenors, or both sections. With a fine choir, it is conceivable that it be sung by all parts in unison since the highest pitch is brief, approached by step, involves the "oo" vowel, comes only once, and is sung *forte*.

The range is a ninth as well for "They Cast Their Nets." The tessitura is lower, allowing any of the voice parts to manage it with relative ease at a moderate dynamic level.

The flexible melody of "Arise, My Love" is best for solo voice. The frequent leaps and tonal shifts require a trained voice. The range is a tenth, and the tessitura shifts from moderate to relatively high.

A range of just an octave and a medium tessitura makes "This is the Day" ideal for choir in unison with full chordal accompaniment. Basses should have no difficulty with the high D's at this dynamic level.

Active and Passive tones

In tonal music, some tones give the impression of being "active," moving toward a goal. Other tones seem to give the feeling of rest. They are the tones that are the goal of the motion. In the major and minor scales, degrees 1, 3, and 5 are often "passive" tones, while all others, including chromatically altered pitches, are "active." Scale degree 4 often resolves to 3, 6 to 5, and 2 to 1. Scale degree 7, the leading tone, resolves up to 8 (1).

It is helpful to represent these tendancies with *moveable do solfège: fa-mi, la-sol, re-do, ti-do* in major; *fa-me, le-sol, ti-do* in minor. The melodic minor scale exhibits tendancies of degrees 6 and 7 depending on melodic direction: a rising melodic line is most likely to proceed *sol-la-ti-do*, while a descending line will proceed *do-te-le-sol*. The harmonic minor is nothing more than the tones of the i, iv, and V triads strung together. The augmented interval from *le* to *ti* should be avoided—unless the music uses a mode other than major or minor, such as music of India or the Middle East. Tones that are highly "charged," such as *ti* and *le* should not be abandoned before being resolved. Avoid using *ti* as the highest pitch in the melody or *le* as the lowest.

Chromatically altered tones are found in secondary dominant chords, in modulations, and in the "blue notes" of African-American music and jazz. A useful rule, one that is easy to follow, is: resolve notes by half step in the direction of the alteration. For example, an F♯ in the key of C usually belongs to a D or D7 chord, and it should resolve up to G; an E♭ in the key of F is likely part of an F7 chord, and it should resolve down to D.

Steps and leaps

In stepwise motion, the energy of each tone is absorbed by the next note. With a leap, however, we tend to combine the notes into a harmonic interval. We perceive the notes at the beginning of "The Star-spangled Banner" as members of a chord. The beginning of "Joy to the World" does not give a harmonic impression. The first phrase of "Arise, My Love" leaves the harmonic impression of a Dmaj7, which must be consonant with the accompaniment. A skilled composer takes into account the aural harmonic impact of leaps when writing them. Two leaps in the same direction should be suspect if their combination clashes with the prevailing harmony.

In an ascending or descending line, it is better to leap first, then step, as shown in the example below. Avoid making a leap from a note that is not part of the harmony or makes a dissonance with other parts.

Ex. 5-7 Movement in one direction involving a leap.

In a) above, the G creates a dissonant fourth with the D be-low. It disagrees with the implied D major harmony. In c) the implied harmony is F to C. The G in the melody does not agree with the harmony, and it creates a dissonant ninth with the F be-low. The leaps in b) and d) are consonant with the implied harmony.

After a large leap (a sixth or larger), the melody normally moves in the opposite direction by step as shown in Ex. 5-8 below. Ex. 5-9, however, shows an exception to this principle due to the contemporary style and the fact that it is enclosed within an octave figure.

Ex. 5-8 Melodic movement following a large leap.

> Melodic writing in contemporary styles may call for more disjunct motion. The melody shown in Ex. 5-9 is from a cantata that makes use of quartal and secondal harmony. The highest note in the melody acts like an inverted pedal point.

Ex. 5-9 Excerpt from *Canticle of the Sun* by Harold Owen.

Unifying and Diversifying elements

We pointed out in Chapter 1 that any melody should have a balance of unifying and diversifying elements. Some of the most important unifying elements are repetition, sequence, and development of a limited number of motives. Diversifying elements are variation, contrasting musical ideas, and changes in register, dynamics, or tonal center.

Repetition plays an important part in Ex. 5-1. The first two phrases are repeated at the end to form an A-B-A structure. In Ex. 5-3 a five-note figure beginning in measure 11 is repeated in cross-rhythm to the meter.

Sequences and motivic development are evident in all of the examples, most notably in Ex. 5-2, where the first phrase is given three sequences, all of them slightly varied.

Contrast is provided by the middle section of Ex. 5-1 which moves to a new key, has new motives, and reaches a dynamic climax. In Ex. 5-3 the phrase beginning in measure 11 provides a contrast to the earlier phrases. In Ex. 5-4 a contrast is made by the repetition of the word "rejoice." Diversity in Ex. 5-2 is more subtle: the variation of the sequence and the hemiola in measure 7.

In all of the examples, the rhythm moves the melody forward toward the ends of the phrases. This is especially true of Ex. 5-2 and 5-4 in which the phrases begin with the feeling of *anacrusis* or up-beat, moving forward toward the next down beat.

Setting text

A primary rule in setting text is to match word stresses with musical stresses. Once you have your text, it is a good idea to write it out in poetic form with hyphens between syllables. Mark the accented syllables in some way. Underlining is a simple method:

They cast their <u>nets</u> in <u>Gal</u> - i - <u>lee</u>

just off the <u>hills</u> of <u>brown</u>;

such hap - py <u>sim</u> - ple <u>fish</u> - er <u>folk</u>

be - <u>fore</u> the <u>Lord</u> came <u>down</u>.

The underlined words should get musical stresses. The list on page 56 shows how notes are given stresses. Another excellent way to stress important words is to use a melisma—two or more notes sung to one syllable (see Ex. 5-4, measure 5).

Seeing the text written out in poetic form will help you to decide on a formal plan. The stanza above can be set as a period with cadence points at "brown" and "down." A half cadence (sometimes called a "progressive cadence") could be used at "brown," and a full cadence at "down."

Once the formal plan has been chosen, you should read through the text to get a sense of meter and rhythm. This particular text could be read in a sing-songy doggerel style:

Such a rhythmic setting would be very unfortunate. Compare it with the rhythm of Ex. 5-2. The half notes, the meter changes, the short melismas, and the hemiola have been used for the sake of variety while maintaining the forward motion. The phrase units are of different sizes, and the music for line 3 of the text continues without pause into the next line. Composers today prefer this kind of asymmetry to the doggerel-like four-by-four symmetry of nursery rhymes and tin pan alley.

There are three distinctive kinds of text setting governed by the ratio of syllables to notes. 1) chant recitation, 2) syllabic setting, and 3) melismatic setting. In chant recitation, many syllables are sung to a single tone. The ancient psalm and canticle tones are examples.

Ex. 5-10 Typical chant formula with reciting tones.

Lord, now lettest thou thy servant depart in peace   * according   to thy word.

Syllabic setting gives each syllable its own note, as in the hymn excerpt in Ex. 5-11.

Ex. 5-11 Typical hymn with syllabic text setting.

The   an - gel Ga - bri - el   from hea - en   came_____

Melismatic text setting assigns several notes to some syllables, as in the Kyrie chant excerpt, Ex. 5-12.

Ex. 5-12 Chant with melismatic text setting.

The more words in the text, the more likely it is that you will use syllabic or chant recitation text setting. Texts with fewer syllables allow more melismatic settings. Beginning composers tend to choose syllabic text setting, but some use of melisma enlivens and varies the texture. If a shorter text is chosen, you not only have the possibility of using melisma, you can repeat important text phrases. Repetition can intensify the importance of words or phrases. The repetition of "we will rejoice" in Ex. 5-4 brings intensity to the climax in measure 5.

A single verse of a hymn, a short prayer or collect, a verse or two of a psalm, or a biblical quotation make excellent texts for short anthems. Even a setting of a mass section (Kyrie, Gloria, Sanctus) can serve as an anthem. A hybrid of syllabic and melismatic text setting is best for anthems of this type.

If you wish to write your own text, make sure it is lyrical and stands up to reading aloud. "O Paraclete, superlative intelligence, propitiator of sins, sacrificial Lamb, vouchsafe us remission of our sins and iniquities" would make a very poor anthem text. "O Lamb of God, you take away the sin of the world. Grant us your peace" would serve much better.

Service Music

The service provides a wealth of opportunities for original music; including the call to worship or introit at the beginning of the service; the "amen" or choral benediction at the conclusion; psalm settings, canticles, the Peace, sections of the Ordinary of the Mass or of the Communion Service, choral responses, gradual verses, and offertory sentences.

Psalms

The Psalms appear in just about every kind of worship service. They can be read or sung responsively by lector and congregation. They can be sung by the choir alone, but in many churches, the people in the pews prefer to participate. The traditional way of singing psalms was to sing them in unison using the psalm tones; a number of simple formulae similar to that shown in Ex. 5-10, or Anglican Chants, short harmonized progressions. Although the traditional methods are still used, newer traditions have evolved, including verses sung by a cantor with a response sung after each verse by the congregation, or a harmonized setting of the verses sung by the choir with an antiphon, sung in unison by the congregation after each verse. The response tune must be simple, easy to read and remember.

Ex. 5-13 is a setting of Psalm 142, "Voce mea ad Dominum." The congregation begins by singing the refrain, accompanied by piano or organ. The choir sings each verse in chant recitation that is in a quasi Anglican Chant style, followed by the refrain, and then ending with the refrain.

The refrain shows two parts, both of which will be sung by the choir with the congregation. The congregation will probably sing only the top part, which is perfectly acceptable. The verses may be printed with music, or with text only in the service leaflet.

The harmonic progression for the verses comes to somewhat of a climax in the third measure, then relaxes to a half cadence before the response returns. This style of psalm singing has proven very successful, since the choir is involved with the verses and the music for the congregation is simple and effective. As the psalm continues, the congregation will remember the refrain and sing it confidently.

Mass sections

Today, churches that celebrate the *Eucharist,* the mass or communion service, do not use musical settings of all of the sections of the Ordinary. The Gloria and the Sanctus are the sections most often sung by all. The Kyrie and the Agnus Dei may be sung by the congregation, but they are sometimes sung by the choir alone. The Credo is seldom sung on a regular basis. The text of the Kyrie ("Lord, have mercy"), is brief, and so musical settings of it are usually very melismatic. Settings of the Gloria are usually syllabic. The Sanctus, Benedictus, and Agnus Dei are often a blend of syllabic and melismatic treatment.

Ex. 5-14 is a modern, but conservative SATB a cappella setting of the Agnus Dei in English. A moderately good volunteer choir should have little difficulty with the piece. The texture is imitative. The mode at the beginning is Mixolydian. For the final phrase, the mode changes to Aeolian, and the dynamic level changes to *pianissimo.*

Ex. 5-13 Psalm 142, *Voce mea ad Dominum* for choir and congregation.

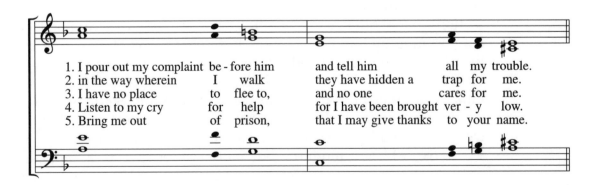

Ex. 5-14 *Agnus Dei* from *Rite II Mass* by the Author.

9
pp
Lamb of God, you take a - way the
pp
Lamb of God, you take a - way the
pp
Lamb of God, you take a -
pp
Lamb of God, you take a -
pp

13
sins of the world: grant us peace.
sins of the world: grant us peace.
way the sins of the world: grant us peace.
way the sins of the world: grant us peace.

Responses

If the people in your congregation enjoy spoken responses, they may also enjoy singing some of them. Familiar responses such as "Amen," "and also with you," "Glory to you, Lord Christ," and "Thanks be to God" can be set with a simple tune for the congregation, with harmony parts for the choir.

The following example is a setting of a dismissal response. The congregation sings the melody, the choir sings in four parts, and the organ (or piano or guitar, etc.) accompanies the singing. Chord symbols are included for guitar. In a contemporary modal style such as this, the fifths in the last two measures are permissible, and the use of seventh chords is common.

Ex. 5-15 Dismissal response.

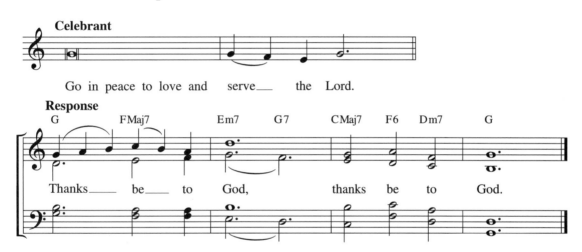

Composing Anthems

If you are trying your hand at writing an anthem for the first time, a good choice is the strophic anthem. In this type of anthem, several verses are set to the same tune, but each verse is treated in a different manner.

Ex. 5-16 is the anthem from which the tune of Ex. 5-2 is taken. Each of the four verses has its own treatment: Verse 1 is in unison, Verse 2 gives the tune to the male voices with two-part chords (dyads) in the soprano and alto, Verse 3 shifts the tune to the women's parts accompanied by dyads in the tenor and bass, Verse 4 presents the tune in imitation with a slight extension for the final cadence. The climax is reached in Verse 4 at "strife closed in the sod," then "peace" is finally secured at the end.

Ex. 5-16 Anthem: "They Cast Their Nets" by the Author.

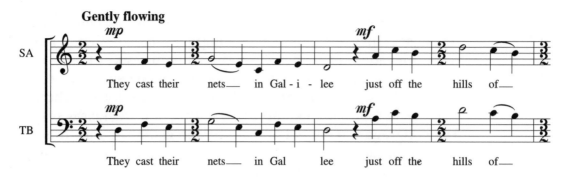

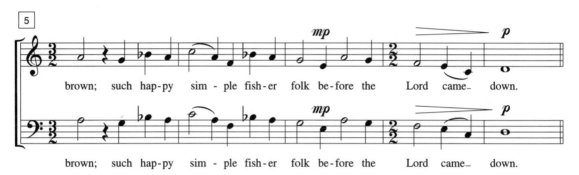

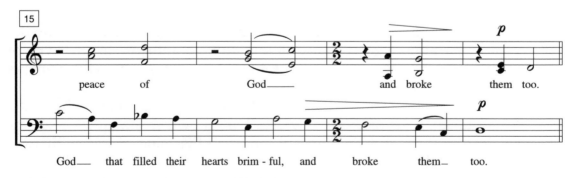

Text: William Alexander Percy, 1885-1942; © Edward B. Marks Music Corp. Used by permission.

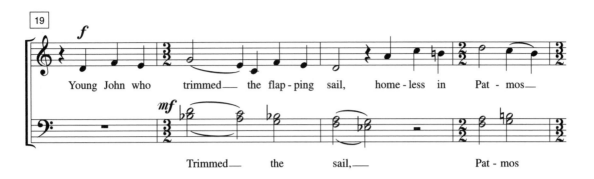

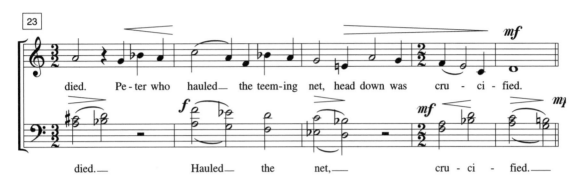

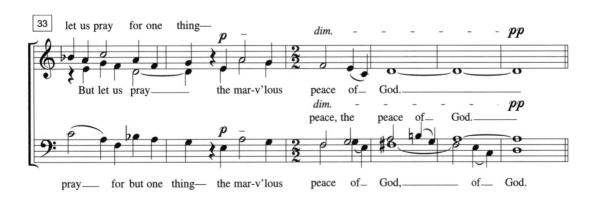

Many anthems are through-composed, such as Mozart's "Ave Verum Corpus." Originally scored for chorus, strings, and continuo, it develops motives as it moves forward. The instruments give a short introduction, an interlude after the first verse of text, and a short coda at the end. Otherwise they substantially double the voice parts. "O Lord, Increase My Faith," attributed to Orlando Gibbons, is also through-composed. The text is a prayer that is in prose. It is syllabic, with some melismas.

The verse anthem, popular in England throughout the seventeenth century, is a type that, unfortunately, is seldom used by composers today. In it, sections for solo voices alternate with sections for chorus that are varied repetitions of the music for the solos. Purcell's "Rejoice in the Lord Alway" is of this type.

Choral textures

A variety of choral textures are used in anthems. Briefly summarized, they are:

1. *Monophonic*, various kinds of doubling
2. Note against note or *homorhythmic* texture
3. *Polyphonic*, with imitative entries
4. *Homophonic*, with melody and accompaniment
5. Call and answer, or antiphonal
6. Hybrids of the above
7. Textures with instrumental accompaniment

Beginning composers will think first of hymn style, where all parts move in the same rhythm. This texture is very common for short anthems. Longer ones, however, demand some relief from homorhythmic texture. Unison singing can be done in several ways, not only with all parts singing the same music. Any section alone, women's voices alone, men's voices alone, high voices (soprano and tenor) or low voices (alto and bass) allow for variety in doubling. One kind of doubling that is not recommended, however, is soprano and alto in octaves, tenor and bass in octaves, or sopranos and basses two octaves apart. The reason for this is that the high voices will be in a relatively high register, and the low voices will be in a low register, making for a poor blend.

Polyphonic textures are enjoyable to hear and fun to sing. The text may become unintelligible, however. Polyphonic settings work well when the text is being repeated, since the listeners have already heard it. If the text is very well known, or if there are just a few syllables, contrapuntal texture will not obscure the text. For this reason, polyphonic textures tend to be more melismatic than others.

When one part carries the melody and the main text, the other parts can provide an accompaniment. Too often, novice composers will resort to "ah" or humming for the accompanying parts. A better plan is to use important words or phrases from the text itself, or words that provide a commentary on the text. Although much of the time the sopranos will receive the melody accompanied by the others, there is no reason why the other parts cannot have the principal role.

Responsorial texture gives a feeling of spaciousness. In an anthem, for example, the tenors might sing a phrase answered by the rest of the choir. Another possibility is two duets taking turns. Josquin Desprez was fond of this texture. Antiphonal ef-ects involving two choirs have always been exciting. With a small choir, the effect can be accomplished by a solo quartet alternating with the whole choir or the choir alternating with instruments or keyboard.

Anthems of moderate length are likely to use many of these textures in the same piece, and various hybrids are possible. A chordal rendition of a phrase of text followed by the same text in a polyphonic treatment can be very effective.

There is something very pure and engaging about a cappella singing, but many smaller church choirs simply cannot sing without accompaniment, except for singing in unison. It is often due to a lack of balance among parts, but it may also be due to lack of skill or rehearsal time. Some publishers provide a keyboard reduction of the choral parts and indicate "for rehearsal only." Others use the indication "for discreet support of voices." In any case, it is perfectly acceptable for the piano or organ to help with some parts or to double all parts in the background. Remember that the keyboard may double vocal parts, but it also may be independent of them. Compared to the choral parts, the accompaniment may have more motion in the form of figuration, or less motion in the form of widely spaced chords. Remember also that an introduction will give the choir their pitches and set the tempo and the spirit of the anthem.

Before you begin working on the composition of a new anthem, consider your singers—their best qualities and their limitations. Consider the text and how it can suggest melodic contours, the location of the climax, and a possible form. Consider ways of setting text, remembering that you can use melismas in strategic places. Consider the various choral textures at your disposal. Consider the possibility of instrumental accompaniment. Consider the people who will hear your new anthem— then get to work!

CHAPTER 6. Notation

Through more than ten centuries, composers have been developing a complex and comprehensive way to communicate their music to performers. Certain standards and conventions have evolved that are instantly recognized by all performers. Since the purpose of the notation is to translate the composer's ideas and wishes into artistic musical performance in the most efficient manner, it is essential that composers have a complete knowledge of standard music notation.

Standard Notation

Use the following questions as a self-test. Then look at Ex. 6-1 to see if your answers agree with what you find there. Can you see ways to improve your own notation? Church musicians come from varied backgrounds of musical training. You will find some of the questions have obvious answers, but that some may challenge your knowledge.

Score items

1. *What element in the notation indicates which performers are to play or sing together? How are the parts named in the score? What is the purpose of brackets and braces? When is a barline not used before the clef on a staff?*
2. *What is the top-to-bottom order for voices? for instruments? for combinations of voices and instruments?*
3. *Which clefs are used for voice types? for orchestral instruments? for keyboard instruments? How and where are clef changes indicated?*
4. *Where does the key signature reside relative to the time signature? Which of these should be displayed on every line or system?*
5. *Where do the tempo indications and metronome markings appear relative to the staff elements? What time value should be used in a metronome marking?*
6. *When should bar lines be drawn through more than one staff? When should they be drawn only on single staves?*

7. *Where are the names of composer, arranger, writer of the lyrics located?*

8. *How do you indicate a change of meter in the middle of a system? at the beginning of a system? How do you show a change of key signature in the middle of a system? at the beginning of a system?*

9. *Why are measure numbers used? Where in the score are the best places to show them? Where are they placed in instrumental parts?*

Staff items

1. *What governs the spacing and alignment of notes and rests?*

2. *What are the rules for stem direction a) for a single line on a staff, b) for two parts on one staff that have the same rhythm, and c) for two parts on one staff that have different rhythms?*

3. *What are the rules for tie placement and direction for a), b), and c) above? for slurs and phrase marks?*

4. *What are the rules for the placement of rests?*

5. *Where are dynamic markings (**mf**, cresc., etc.) located for single-line instruments, for keyboards, for voices?*

6. *Where are articulations, embellishment symbols, fermatas, and bowing marks placed relative to notes?*

7. *How are notes that are only a step apart notated a) on a single stem, b) in chords and clusters, and c) when two independent parts that share a staff are a step apart?*

8. *What governs the use of beams and flags?*

9. *How are tuplets (triplets, quintuplets, etc.) notated?*

Lyrics and text items

1. *Where do lyrics go in two-staff hymnal style? in open choral score? in the case of divisi parts on a single staff?*

2. *How are words with more than one syllable shown?*

3. *How are syllables treated that are sung to a melisma?*

4. *How is punctuation used in a lyric? in humming or neutral vowel sounds?*

5. *How is spoken text shown?*

6. *How are translations of languages other than English handled?*

7. *How do you indicate a solo part? If two instruments share a single staff, how do you indicate which is to play the given notes?*

Ex. 6-1 Beginning measures of "Chorale and Alleluia" by the Author.

Chorale and Alleluia

Notating score items

A single line at the left joins all staves of vocal and instrumental parts that sound together. Amateurs sometimes neglect to draw this line, or they draw a large curly brace instead. This leads to confusion, especially when some parts are not involved in a system and do not get a staff. Brackets and braces define groupings, such as chorus, wind instruments, and organ manuals. Take note, in Ex. 6-1, that the Soprano Solo part has no bracket. Individual instrumental parts, such as the flute part, will have neither left line nor bracket. A curvy brace is used for keyboards, and the instrument name is located to the left of the central point of the brace.

The first system is indented, and the full names of all parts are given at the left. Transposing instruments should have their home key included (Horn in F, for example) on the first system. On subsequent systems, part names are abbreviated. Transposing parts are usually written as they appear in the parts, but some scores show all parts in concert pitch. It is essential in this case to indicate on the first page of the score that it is a C score—not transposed.

The order of parts from top to bottom generally follows the order for a full orchestra—woodwinds first, then horns, then trumpets and trombones, tuba, timpani, percussion, harp, piano, any featured soloist's part, and strings. When the score calls for organ, it is usually placed at the bottom. In each orchestra section, instruments are given from highest to lowest. Choral parts are also ordered from highest to lowest, but a solo vocal part that is more than just a few measures appears above the choral parts. When a chorus is accompanied by instruments, the choral parts are generally at the top except for large orchestral scores, where they appear above the strings. Keyboard parts are at the bottom (except when the keyboard is the prime soloist, as in a concerto). For chorus with an obligato part, such as a flute, it is usually placed above the choral parts. Guitar parts are usually below the choral parts. Handbell parts may appear above or below the choral parts, and a staff showing the pitches of the bells required appears above the first system. A small ensemble may use orchestra score order or may arrange parts from highest to lowest. For example, a score for flute, viola, harp, and chorus may appear in that order—or flute, viola, then chorus, then harp—or chorus at the top, then flute, viola, and harp.

In open score, sopranos and altos use treble clef, tenors use the treble clef with an 8 attached below it, and basses use bass clef. When the music is simple enough to appear on two staves, the sopranos and altos share the treble clef, and the tenors and basses share the bass clef. Tenors are expected to read either the modern vocal tenor clef or bass clef. Flutes, oboes, clarinets, trumpets, bells, xylophone, vibraphone, and violins use treble clef exclusively. Bassoons, trombones, tubas, cellos, and string basses use bass clef, but bassoons, trombones, and cellos may also use tenor clef or even treble clef for high parts. Violas use the alto clef, but very high parts may take them into treble clef. Do not use treble clef unless the music stays above the top line of the alto staff. Horns use bass clef only for very low parts. Some bass clarinet parts are written in bass clef, but they usually read in the treble clef, as do saxophones of all sizes. Marimba may be written on one or two staves, harp, piano, organ, and other keyboard instruments use two staves (often three for organ). Most guitar parts are written in treble clef with the understanding that the music will sound an octave lower. The vocal tenor clef is becoming more and more common for guitar, and we recommend its use.

Clef changes may be needed in the middle of a measure. Since they take up space, a corresponding space should be left in all other parts at that point in order to maintain vertical alignment. If the first note of a measure is to be in a new clef, the clef itself appears at the end of the previous measure. If the first note in the new clef appears at the beginning of a new system, the clef appears at the end of the previous system *after* the bar line. Clefs that indicate a change are about 75% the size of the normal clefs.

When there is a key signature, it appears just to the right of the clef in every system. The time signature or meter appears only in the first measure and at places where it changes. When a new key signature begins in the first measure of a system, it is shown at the end of the previous system after the bar line. In older scores, the signature was canceled with naturals before the new one appeared. This practice has fallen out of use today. However, if the change is to a key without a signature, it is necessary to cancel the old key signature. A double bar to the left of the new key signature helps to call attention to it.

Tempo directions (Largo, Fast, etc.) are placed above the top part. In large ensemble scores, they may appear above major sections, especially the strings. The first tempo indication is aligned with the meter sign. If a metronome marking is used, it follows right after the tempo indication. The note used should be equal to the conductor's beat. Tempo change items (rit., accel, etc.) go below the staff for instruments, above for voices.

Bar lines for choral parts are drawn only on the staves in order to leave plenty of room for the lyrics. Instrumental groups, such as the wood winds in Ex. 6-1, have bar lines drawn through the whole group. Keyboard instruments, harp, and marimba have bar lines drawn through both staves. Most organ parts have a bar line through the staves for the manuals with independent ones for the pedals.

The names of composer, arranger, and transcriber appear right-justified above the end of the first staff. The source of the lyrics (Biblical quotations, poets, writers, translators, etc.) appear left-justified at the left margin above the tempo indication.

Measure numbers are needed for convenience in rehearsal. We suggest that they be used above the top part in all but the first system, enclosed in a box. In larger scores, they may appear above major instrumental groups. Other possibilities are every five or ten bars, or at important musical junctures. Rehearsal letters can be useful in very large works. We suggest that measure numbers in instrumental parts be placed at the left of each staff without enclosures.

Notating staff items

Rhythmic spacing should be roughly proportional to note values. Longer note values take more space than shorter ones. Spacing relative to the beat in the measure is also useful. Notes that sound together must be vertically aligned. Poorly spaced or aligned scores cause a lot of wasted time and anxiety in rehearsals. Crowded or too widely spaced notation should be avoided. We will have more to say about this subject in the discussion of computer-generated notation.

With too many composers, handwritten scores often break the rules for stem direction. Although most computer notation programs handle stem direction properly, some cases will require special attention. For one part on a single staff, notes above the third line have down stems, and notes below the third line have up stems. Notes on the third line should "go with the flow" of adjacent notes. With beamed groups, stems are up if more notes are below the third line, down if more notes are above the third line. In the case of chords, stem direction depends on how far from the third line the top and bottom notes are. For example, a chord in the treble clef consisting of first space F, middle line B, fourth line D will take an up stem. The F is three steps below the middle line (−3), and D is two steps above the middle line (+2). As a result (−1), an up-stem is needed. An oc-tave consisting of first space F (-3) and top line F (+4) will need a down stem (+1).

When two parts share the same staff but have the same rhythm, only one set of stems is required. When these parts have independent rhythms, they must have opposing stems. Ex.

6-2 demonstrates stem direction for a) a single part or a unison part, b) two parts with the same rhythm, and c) two parts that have different rhythms. Note the displacement of the quarter rests and the need for two whole notes in c).

Ex. 6-2 Stem, tie, and slur direction; placement of dynamics and articulations.

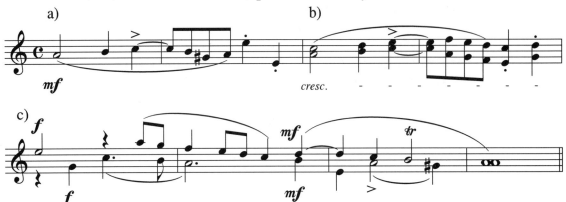

Ties are drawn between note heads. For single notes on a staff, the tie curves up for down-stems as in a) above, down for up-stems. In tied chords, the outer ties are drawn in opposite direction, as in b) above. The inner notes in chords have ties that are parallel to the closest outer note. For two independent parts on a single staff, ties are drawn in the same direction as the stems as in c) above. Slurs and phrase marks are usually on the note side. For two parts on a staff, they are on the stem or beam side and oppose each other, as in c) above.

Rests other than whole and half are located in the middle of the staff except when they are in independent parts as shown in Ex. 6-2 c). The whole rest hangs from the fourth line and takes the size of a complete measure, except in meters larger than $\frac{4}{4}$.

Dynamic markings and expressive text items such as *dolce, marcato,* or *espressivo* appear below the notes for single-line instruments and between the staves for keyboards. They appear above the notes for vocal music in order to make room for the lyrics. If two parts share the same staff, expression marks will appear above for the upper part and below for the lower part. When two choral parts share one staff, the lyrics for the upper part must be above the notes, and expression marks will be both above and below the staff somewhat offset from the base line of the lyrics (see Ex. 5-16, measures 30-38).

Articulations (staccato marks, accents, trills, fermatas, etc.) are most often placed on the note side, except as shown in Ex. 6-2 c).

Chords with the interval of a second pose a problem because there is not room enough to align them vertically.

When they are on a single stem, the upper note is on the right and the lower on the left of the stem. Ex. 6-3 shows proper notation of seconds when a) they are on a single stem and b) when they are in adjacent parts sharing a single staff. Notes a second apart in two independent parts on a staff should have their stems aligned. Consequently, the upper note must be on the left and the lower on the right (see b) below).

Tone clusters present an especially difficult problem for hand-written notation. When three notes occupy successive steps, the middle note is moved to the other side of the stem (see a) below, measures 4 and 5).

Ex. 6-3 Seconds in various configurations .

Beams are used to show groupings of notes which conform to the meter and to the conductor's beat. In common time, beamed groups usually show each beat. Four eighths may be beamed together to show each two beats. Examine the beamed groups in Ex. 1-1. You will see that there is no beaming across beat 3. Unusual beaming may be used when there is a cross rhythm, such as eighth notes beamed in groups of 3+3+2.

In triple meter, when the tempo is relatively slow, beamed groups will conform to the beat. Ex. 5-1 demonstrates this. In faster tempo, six eighth notes may be grouped together, as in Ex. 4-7 where the beat is actually one to the bar. In $\frac{6}{8}$ meter, beamed groups will indicate two beats per bar, as in Ex. 2-1. Flags are used when an eighth note (or shorter) can not be beamed with others in a group. Sometimes a flag will be used to denote a break in the phrase.

The term *tuplet* is used for subdivisions such as duplets, triplets, quadruplets, etc. Ex. 6-4 shows several ways to indicate tuplets: a) brackets with numbers, recommended for notes without beams, b) numbers alone, when beams show grouping, c) number with bracket, useful for larger tuplets, d) number with broken bracket, e) numbers that can be omitted after the first few triplets when it is obvious that triplets will continue, f) tuplet shown as a ratio—7 in the space of 6, and g) numbers with slurs, an older style not recommended because the slurs can be confused with articulation markings.

Ex. 6-4 Tuplets in various configurations .

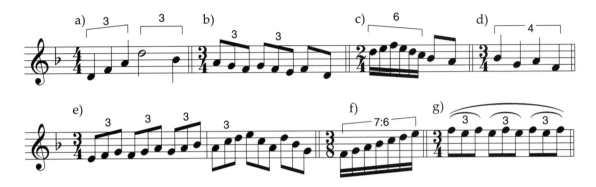

Transcribing lyrics

Hymns and simple four-part choral music may be scored on two staves with women's parts in treble clef and men's parts in bass clef. As long as the lyric is the same for all parts, it can be centered between the staves. The verses in Psalm 142, Ex. 5-13, are scored this way. Simple melody with accompaniment or two-part polyphony can also be scored this way. Ex. 5-16 demonstrates this. Four-part open score is recommended for more complex or polyphonic music, such as the *Agnus Dei*, Ex. 5-14. The lyrics are provided for all parts. For a cappella music, a keyboard reduction is recommended. When the chorus expands to more parts through divisi, it may be necessary to add staves or to show lyrics both above and below the staff.

Beaming is the same for vocal music as for instrumental music. Using flags for each syllable is no longer standard. The rules for text underlay are quite simple: Each syllable is centered beneath the note to which it is sung. Hyphens are used between syllables of a polysyllabic word. In the case of melismas, the syllable is left-justified directly below the first note of the melisma. If the melismas continues with many notes, extra hyphens may be inserted sparingly until the next syllable arrives. For a melisma on a single syllable or the last one of a word, a base-line extension is drawn until it reaches the last note of the melisma. Melismas are usually given a slur as well. The hyphens, word extensions, and slurs in Ex. 5-14 adhere to these principles.

Singers need to see the complete syllable under the first note of a melisma in order to pronounce the word correctly, in spite of the fact that the final consonants will be delayed until the end. Ex. 6-5 shows some potential problems that can occur when a composer tries to show how the words will actually be sung.

Ex. 6-5 Potential lyric problems.

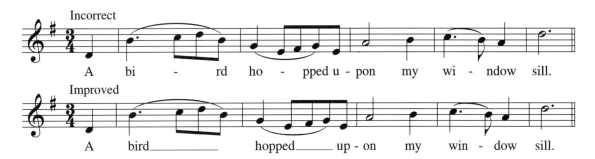

When composing or arranging a choral piece, you must be careful to use the punctuation and capitalization exactly as it appears in the source text. If words or phrases of the text are repeated, be sure to set them off by commas (see Ex. 5-4). It is recommended that you print the text as it appears in its original form on a separate page from the score, especially if it is a poem. It is very helpful to the performers and conductor to see it displayed this way and to read it for its meaning and intrinsic lyrical qualities.

Expressions, such as "alleluia," or "amen," as well as accompanying sounds such as "ah," "oh," or humming, are treated as if they were sentences. The first appearance is capitalized, and any repetitions are set off by commas (see Ex. 6-1).

Spoken text or non-vocal sounds (hand claps, finger snaps, etc.) call for an x in place of the usual note heads. A problem arises when the rhythm calls for half notes or larger. One solution for this is to use large note heads with an x inside.

Other text items

When the text is not in English, it is helpful to provide a translation, except perhaps for the most common liturgical texts such as the *Agnus Dei*. The translations can be given in the notes on a page before the score begins. If a competent transliteration is available, the English text can be underlaid below the non-English text, preferably in italics. This allows a chorus to sing in English if the original text is not appropriate to the occasion.

Solo parts within a chorus must be carefully indicated. If a short solo occurs within a section of the chorus, it can be indicated above the staff by the word "Solo." When the whole section is to resume, the word "Tutti" or "All" should appear. Longer solos are notated in a staff above the chorus (see Ex. 6-1).

For instrumental parts that share a staff on the score, the following indications should be used:

1.	First player plays alone.
2.	Second player plays alone.
a2	Two players play the part in unison.
1. solo	First player has an important solo.

Using a Computer for Notation

The computer has become a valuable tool for composers. Notation programs allow composers to produce camera-ready scores in much less time than it takes to make hand-written scores. In addition, the computer is able to play your scores in real time, giving you a very helpful way of checking for errors, as well as a good idea of the effect of the work in real time. The computer is able to extract parts quickly and accurately as well.

In spite of these advantages, there are serious potential problems facing composers using a computer. Among these are the following:

1. The best computer notation programs do not know everything there is to know about standard notation. The composer must know not only the correct use and placement of notes, rests, signatures, ties, slurs, tuplets, articulations, dynamic markings, tempo markings, and other music symbols; he or she must have a good eye for formatting, proper font, size, and style for all textual items, know the special requirements of the singers or instrumentalists, and anticipate the requirements for presentation of the score for publication.

2. A well-trained composer should be able to produce a score by hand. This means that he or she must understand the principles behind the choices that the computer notation program routinely makes, including those which must be countermanded in special cases.

3. We recommend that composers write a first draft in pencil *away* from the computer, rather than compose *at* the computer. The nature of synthesizer input and the computer's easy routines for copying, transposing, and doubling can lead

the composer into easy solutions, and the playback, while accurate in terms of pitch and rhythm, cannot replicate the subtle nuances of dynamics, tempo, and tone quality of live performers. In addition, the computer is capable of executing complicated rhythms and enormous leaps in pitch that live musicians cannot hope to manage. Composers need to realize that the tempo they assign is very likely to be much too fast for live performance.

4. Since the computer can play constantly and tirelessly with no rest, composers working at the computer tend to write con-inuous music, ignoring the need for rests and for breathing—not only physical breathing by singers and wind players, but for the need of the music to breathe (phrasing, tension and release).

If you are serious about composing and arranging for your church musicians, you should choose a notation program carefully. There are several products available for the casual amateur costing from about $50 to $250. These will not do for your needs. They are too limited, and they are likely to make wrong decisions. Sophisticated notation programs such as *Finale* (used in this book), *Sibelius,* and *Igor* (a promising new program) are better choices. These programs range in price from about $300 to $1500 or more. At the present time, the majority of church musicians are using *Finale*.

Below you will find a chart that gives examples of various text items in a score with suggestions for font, size, style, and position.

SUGGESTED FORMATTING FOR TEXT ITEMS

NOTE: In the font column, "Music font" designates the font used by your notation program. The music font used in this book is *Maestro*. In the size column, "F" indicates fixed point size. The point size remains the same no matter what percentage is used for the score. "V" designates varying point size. The point size varies with the percentages used for the score.

Item	Examples (F: @ 100%; V: @ 85%)	Font	Size	Style	Justification and location
Title	Sanctus	Times or Palatino	18-24 F	Plain	Centered near top of page
Subtitle	SATB, a cappella SAB and Piano	Times or Palatino	12-14 F	Plain	Centered beneath title

Composer or arranger	Henry Purcell Hugo Distler Arr. by Jon Starke	Times or Palatino	10-12 F (14V)	Plain	Right justified, above last bar, first system
Lyrics	Be thou my vision	Times	12-14V	Plain	Centered below notes; left aligned with first note of a melisma
Tempo description	**Allegro vivace** **Tempo Primo** **Meno mosso** **Quietly flowing** **a tempo**	Times	12-14 F (14V for scores at 75% or less)	Bold	First tempo above the meter of highest staff; others above the bar where tempo changes
Metronome mark	(♩ = 120) or (♩ = 120)	Music font for note, Times for text	14F for note, 10F for text	Plain or italic	After tempo description
Measure numbers	36	Helvetica	9-14 V	Plain	Above first bar in each system
Rehearsal letters	A	Times	14-18 F	Bold	Above top staff where needed
Words indicating dynamics, articulation, style, etc.	*cresc.* *leggiero* *simile* *sotto voce* *dolce*	Times	12 V	Italic	For piano: between staves; for instruments: below staff; for voice: above staff
Performance instructions and techniques	divisi Stopped Straight mute pizz. hard mallets	Times	12 V	Plain	Above the staff or above the notes affected
Changing tempo	*rit. - - - - -* *accel. - - - -* *allargando* *stretto* *poco a poco*	Times	12 V	Italic	Usually below or between staves; occasionally above; always above for voice or chorus
Who and how many	tutti a2 1. Solo Change to piccolo	Times	12 V	Plain	Above the staff
Full name of instruments	Bassoon Violins I Harpsichord Timpani Soprano I	Times	12 V	Plain	Left of staff for System 1 only; between staves for grand staff instruments

Abbreviated staff names	Fl. 1, 2 Vla.	Times	10-12 V	Plain	Left of staff for System 2+
Dynamic markings	*mf* *ppp* *sfz* *fff*	Music font	24 V, 20V for voice parts	Plain	Above staff for voice; below for instruments; between for grand staff

Formatting Scores

The examples in this section have been reduced about 15% in order to fit on the page. In the discussion, percentages given suggest settings to use in your notation program.

Choral scores

The most common type of choral score you will encounter is for SATB mixed chorus with either piano accompaniment or piano reduction. Ex. 6-6 is the first page of an anthem for SATB a cappella. Voice parts are indicated as S, A, T, and B. When the keyboard part is a reduction, it is indicated as "Piano (for rehearsal only)." We have reduced the keyboard staves to 75% of the choral staves. This is convenient for keyboard reductions. When the keyboard part is independent, no percentage reduction should be made.

Most published choral music allows for two or three systems per page. We recommend two, since using three systems invites crowding of individual staves. Chorus members can read scores easily set as low as 65% if the text is of a comfortable size. Ex. 6-7 sets the page size at 75%.

A bracket is used for all choral parts. If there is an independent solo part, one that is not within the chorus, it should be located above the choral parts and should not be included in the bracket. Incidental solos within the chorus are indicated on the choral staff by the word "Solo." The word "Tutti" indicates resumption by all singers on that part.

The text should be printed in a font that is easy to read, and the point size should be as large as possible without crowding. Ex. 6-6 uses Times at 12 pt., not fixed. This means that the text will be reduced by the same percentage as the musical score. Fixed size means that the characters are full-sized and are not affected by changes in percentage of the score. The title is Times 24 pt. fixed, the writer and composer are Times 10 pt. fixed, and the tempo marking is Times 12 pt. fixed, bold.

Ex. 6-6 Typical layout for SATB *a cappella* with piano reduction.

Chorale and Alleluia

Harold Owen, b. 1931

Ex. 6-7 is the first page of an anthem for unison voices with keyboard accompaniment. Titles, names, tempo markings, and lyrics are similar in font and point size to Ex. 6-6. In scores for unison voices, the treble clef is used for both men and women. When a section is for men alone, the clef may be changed to bass clef. In this anthem, there are four verses. Verse 3 is for women alone and the scoring is lighter. The final verse is scored for all voices again. The keyboard part is full-sized, not reduced as in Ex. 6-6.

Although there would be space enough for four systems, three are used here to avoid any crowding. In addition, when published, the copyright information would take up space at the bottom, usually three lines of text. Page 2 and above can easily take four systems. Your notation program should allow you to set up system spacing for all pages other than page 1. Then you can adjust the systems to make room for titles, indent for full part names, and text items that occur only on the first page.

The keyboard part is relatively simple and requires only two staves. It can be played on piano, organ, even electronic piano or synthesizer. If you write for organ specifically, you can use two or three staves, depending on the need for the pedal staff. Organ registration is usually left to the discretion of the organist since there is such a variety of instruments that may be used to play the part. Dynamic markings are helpful in that regard.

The first and second verses begin with the same words, but new words for the second verse begin in measure 8. Notice that the verse numbers are vertically aligned as they are in a hymnal. Words that begin a melisma should be left aligned as well (see measure 9).

The bracket on the choral staff indicates that it is for unison voices, not a solo, in which case there would be no bracket.

Some anthems begin with unison voices, then expand to two or more parts later in the piece. It is common to use a layout such as Ex. 6-7 when more staves will be needed later. You should make sure that the notation program you use allows you to do this. In Finale, you begin in Scroll View with the maximum number of staves that you will need. When all of the music is entered, you can "optimize" all systems—remove any unused staves, then set up your final layout. With scores for full orchestra, however, it is customary to show all staves on the first page, even if some of them have only rests.

If a flute obligato part were added to Ex. 6-7, it would be written on a staff placed above the choral line, and there would be no bracket used.

Ex. 6-7 Typical layout for unison chorus with keyboard accompaniment.

BREATHE ON ME, BREATH OF GOD

for Unison Chorus and Keyboard Accompaniment

Edwin Hatch, 1878   Harold Owen

Verse 2 may be sung by men only or as a solo.

When choral parts are simple enough to be written on two staves, women's parts in treble clef on the upper staff, men's parts in bass clef on the lower staff, a keyboard reduction is unnecessary. Ex. 5-16 can be read easily at the piano for rehearsals. The anthem can be sung during the service with light doubling by organ if necessary. The format shows S., A. for the upper staff, T., B. for the lower staff, and a bracket encloses both staves. If the lyrics were the same throughout for all parts, they would appear only between the staves. In our example, the lyrics are given below the lower staff as well because they will continue for tenor and bass in the next verse while the sopranos and altos divide. From bar 30 to the end the parts become more independent, so lyric entries will be needed above and below both staves. If this texture had been used much longer, the score would be expanded to four choral staves (and a reduction might be supplied there as well).

Below is the beginning of the "Phos hilaron" for an evening service. A bracket is used for the choir and congregation's staves but not for the cantor's staff.

Ex. 6-8 Typical layout for choral responses.

The shorter parts for the cantor have shorter staves. If full length staves are used the notes will be spread out too much. The format used in Ex. 5-13 can be used for psalm refrain and verses or for cantor and response as well for cantor at the top rather than the two-part refrain as shown.

Scores for SSA with keyboard or SAB with keyboard may use two or three staves for voices and two for the keyboard. When two staves are used for voices, soprano 1 and soprano 2 share a staff, and alto is on the second staff. For SAB, soprano and alto may share the upper staff and the baritone part is on the second staff.

When chorus is joined by handbells, the score order will depend on the nature and complexity of the handbell parts. When only a few bells are involved, a single staff can be used, and it can be located either above or below the chorus staves. For a large full set of chromatically tuned handbells, two staves may be needed. They are located below the choral staves. A small staff or grand staff as in Ex. 6-9, showing the pitches required, should be placed below the title and above the first system of the score.

Ex. 6-9 Staves showing handbells required for an anthem.

Ex. 6-9 might serve as the introduction to an anthem with handbells. The layout could be used as well for a handbell piece without voices. If the highest bells are not available, the piece will be satisfactory without them.

Instrumental scores

There are many examples in this book that involve keyboard instruments. They adhere to the principles discussed be-low except that many of them have been reduced in size to fit on these pages.

The piano is being used more and more in worship services today, even in churches where there is a fine pipe organ. Although it is likely to be used for accompaniment the piano can also be used for preludes, postludes, or as a "voluntary" during the service.

The curved brace is used for all instruments that read from a grand staff—piano, organ, harpsichord, harp, and celesta are the best known. The marimba is occasionally written on two staves. Page margins may range from 0.5 in. to 1.25 in. We recommend 0.75 in. If the score will be bound or punched for a three-hole binder, the left margin should be about 0.25 in. more than the others for a right-hand page. For double-sided pages, left -hand pages should allow 0.25 in. extra for the right margins.

We recommend a page size of 75% to 85% for keyboard music. The first staff should be indented about a half inch. Four or five systems on the first page should leave room for titles. Subsequent pages can have five or six systems. Be sure to leave enough room between staves of the grand staff for ledger lines, double stemming, phrase marks, and dynamic markings. Space between systems should be larger than the space between staves to allow for high and low notes, phrase markings, major tempo markings, and to help the eye to see the grand staff groupings. Bar lines are drawn through both staves.

Note spacing according to the time signature can be used for simple music that does not have a wide range of note values. The best notation programs allow for spacing by *allotments*, by which notes of shorter values receive proportionately more space than notes of longer values. A measure full of sixteenth notes will be wider than a measure with a single whole note. Be sure to make room for accidentals, for sonorities containing notes a step apart, and for clef changes.

When formatting scores for organ with a pedal staff, you should be able to fit four staves on a page, three on the first page using portrait orientation (11 in. tall, 8.5 in. wide). Many organ works are published in landscape orientation, allowing for three systems per page, two on the first page. Standard organ music has the curved brace on the upper two staves, and the left line connects all three staves. Bar lines are usually drawn through the upper staves (our preference), but some editions draw bar lines through all three staves.

Keyboard music can explore a variety of musical textures, from block chords to multi-voiced polyphony. When a staff con-ains chords or two parts that have the same rhythm, single stems are used. When there are two contrapuntal parts sharing a staff, the upper part's stems are up and lower part's stems are down. When most of the staff is homorhythmic, but a few places have two different rhythms, the double-stemming is used only for those places (see Ex. 6-7, measures 11-15). If the texture is polyphonic, but a few places have the same rhythm, double-stemming should be used throughout (see Ex. 4-8 and 5-14, the keyboard reduction).

When one or more instruments are accompanied by keyboard, the instrumental parts are located above the keyboard staves. If they belong to the same family (e.g. woodwinds, in the case of Ex. 6-1), they are given a bracket. A mixed ensemble such as oboe, trumpet, and cello will not share a bracket. If you are fortunate enough to have a string quartet to play during a service, the four staves will be connected by a bracket.

Tips for *Finale* Users

If you are using another notation program, stay tuned. Some of these tips can be translated easily into the application you are currently using.

Finale has the reputation of being difficult to learn. This may have been true of its earlier versions, but the current versions are much more user-friendly. *Finale* is especially useful for church musicians with several templates provided for various scores that can save you hours of set-up time. The following comments apply to *Finale* 97 and later versions.

Hardware and software needs

Your computer needs plenty of memory and disk space for music files. Although 32 MB of RAM is sufficient, we recommend that you upgrade to 64 MB. Memory upgrades are not expensive, and the added speed and flexibility is well worth the cost. Your hard drive should have at least 500 MB capacity. If you intend to create a large number of scores, you should have 1 or 2 GB, standard for newer computers. *Finale* runs equally well on Windows and Macintosh computers, and there are very few differences in its operation on the two platforms. We strongly recommend that you invest in a laser printer for the best results. 300 dpi (dots per inch) is acceptable, but 600 is better for music notation. *Finale* allows note input from your computer keyboard, but input from a MIDI keyboard is much faster and allows you to monitor playback for editing purposes. You will need a MIDI interface to connect the MIDI keyboard to your computer.

Using templates

Probably the most important advice we can give you at this point is to make use of templates. A template is a formatted blank score of one or two pages with the needed staves, part names, brackets, page percentage, and dummy title, composer, page numbers, and other useful items that need only to be changed for your present needs. *Finale* provides "General Templates" that include many usual combinations including keyboard alone and with solo, and various instrumental ensembles, "choral Templates" including all sorts of vocal ensembles, and "church Templates" including church orchestra, handbells, hymnal, piano and organ, and even shape-note hymnal formats.

Let's say you want to write for SAB and keyboard. Open a new file from the Templates Folder called "SAB with Piano." To do this in *Finale* 97 press Option as you choose Open from the File menu. In *Finale* 98, choose "File from Template" from the File Menu. In *Finale* 2000, choose "New" from the File Menu and "Document from Template" in the submenu. This opens the template as an "Untitled" file, in order to protect the template itself. You can now give your new file a name using "Save As" from the File Menu. You have been saved all the work of setting up the score for each new piece. If you wish to change the template to suit your own requirements, you can make changes in it, then save it with the original template name. The next time you use it, it will appear with your own settings.

You can create your own special templates from scratch. Open a new file and make all the settings you prefer. Save it with the name for your new template in the Templates Folder. It is possible to make a template from an existing file by selecting all measures, pressing Clear, and deleting or changing text blocks. We do not recommend this, however, because the file will still retain data (especially the lyrics and any text or shape expressions you created), and the file will be larger than a template should be.

Music spacing and updating the format

Current versions of *Finale* allow for automatic music spacing. This ensures that various items are considered in music spacing, including accidentals, unisons and seconds, clefs, and lyrics. It is a little disconcerting during note entry, but if you do not use the automatic setting, you should use the music spacing command from time to time to avoid crowding and collisions. Any time you do this, however, you should also update the layout. Much grief and wasted time can be avoided by updating the layout any time you move anything. In general, it is a good idea to update the layout with page one of the score on screen.

Save frequently

The most drastic waste of time happens when you have done hours of work and then there is a power outage or your computer crashes for some reason. If you have not been saving your work on a regular basis, all that effort will be lost and cannot be retrieved. *Finale* offers you an auto-save function which will save your work after an amount of time that you set. This can be very helpful for beginners. You can use "Revert" from the File Menu when your latest operations have resulted in disaster. This takes you back to your last saved version.

A very useful feature of *Finale* is "Multiple Undo." When you have made a mistake, "Undo" will remove it. If you realize that you have made a mistake several operations earlier, you can get the "Undo/Redo Lists" from the Edit Menu, allowing you to return to the place before the mistake occurred.

Setting the time signature

Young musicians have grown up with the faulty information that "the upper number tells how many beats in the measure, and the lower number tells what kind of a note gets the beat." This is a really dangerous half-truth! When you set up your time signature, think first how it will be conducted. If your piece is in $\frac{6}{8}$ meter, it will probably be conducted in two. Set up two beats, each having a value of a dotted quarter. If your meter is $\frac{3}{4}$, but it will be conducted in one beat per bar, set up one dotted half note. If your meter is $\frac{4}{4}$, but you will conduct it in two, set up two beats, each a half note in duration. This will give you a $\frac{2}{2}$ meter or ¢, the *alla breve* sign. Then choose "More Choices," check "Use a different time signature for display," and set that to four quarter notes.

Pick-up bars

Pick-up bars always cause problems for beginners. Here is the quickest and easiest way to set one up: Let's say your piece is in common time, but you have a quarter-note pick-up. The piece will probably be set to common time by default. Now select the first measure with the Time Signature Tool, set the region from Measure 1 to Measure 1, and reduce the number of beats to one. Click on "More Choices," check "Use a different time signature for display," and make sure it is set up for four quarters. Remember that a pick-up bar is not counted as the first measure, so it is necessary to adjust the measure numbers. To do so, choose the Measure Tool, select "Measure Numbers" from the Measure Menu, and "Edit Regions..." In the dialog box that appears, change the first number in the region from 1 to 2.

Lyrics

Lyrics must be easy to read. This means they must be large enough, and they must be free of collisions and crowding. Choral scores should have a page size between 75% and 85%. Times 12-14 pt. is quite readable. If lyrics are included in the music spacing options, there will be no crowding. Occasionally the spacing will be overly skewed by syllables such as "through" followed by a short one such as "a." In such cases, the position of the syllable can be moved left or right a small amount by selecting "Adjust Syllables" in the Lyrics Menu, clicking on the note involved, dragging across the handle, and using the arrow keys for the adjustment. The first syllable of a melisma should begin directly below the first note of the melisma, not center-justified beneath. Use "Adjust Syllables" and the arrow keys to move the syllable.

When entering words of more than one syllable, be sure to enter the last syllable before doing any other typing or adjusting. If you abandon a word before it is completed, a string of hyphens will stretch out to the end of the line and will not go away unless you delete the syllable where the hyphens begin.

When you find you have made typing errors, it is safest to correct them in the Edit Lyrics box. It is helpful to proof-read your lyrics in this box as well.

The Word Extension Plug-in is very useful for entering needed word extensions all at once. You should wait, however, until all formatting has been done before you use the plug-in. When you are ready, choose the Mass Mover Tool, press Command-A (Select All), then apply the plug-in. Remember that where there are word extensions there should be slurs as well.

If you need a hyphen or a space within a word assigned to a single note (such as "e in" in Italian) hold down Option as you type the space or the hyphen.

Ties, slurs, and phrase marks

You will find that ties, slurs, and phrase marks will need the most adjusting. Ties between very short notes tend to be too small, and long ties tend to be too flat. *Finale* allows you to specify every aspect of ties, but it is a daunting task. The Tie Tool (in the Special Tools), however, is easy to use. When making adjustments, use Command-2 to magnify the image. If a tie is entered in the wrong direction, select one of the handles and select "Tie Direction" from the Special Tools Menu to make the change.

Slurs can be applied to note heads or to the measure. Most of the time you will apply them to note heads. A slur between adjacent notes then takes only a double click. If *Finale* draws a slur between notes and you want it on the stem or beam side, the change can be made using Smart Shape Menu/Direction.

Slurs and phrase marks that cross system breaks need to be carefully monitored. Be sure to look at both portions of the interrupted slurs and phrase marks and make adjustments as needed.

Tempo indication and metronome marking

The Text Tool is best for tempo indications and metronome markings because you can specify font, size, and style for each of its parts. If you create the metronome marking in the same text block with the tempo description, they will move together when the position is adjusted. We suggest that you create tempo indications and metronome markings in Scroll View so that they will be attached to the first system and move with it. If they are created in Page view, they do not move when the layout is adjusted.

Cautionary accidentals

One of the rules of standard notation states that an accidental is good throughout the measure, and the bar line cancels it for the next measure. While this may be true, without cautionary accidentals, we would too often forget to cancel an accidental. This is especially true of singers. We suggest an alternate rule: All accidentals must be canceled in the measure after they ap-pear. If the next appearance of the pitch in question is close by or appears after some rests, cancellation is advised. You will notice that care has been taken to provide cautionary accidentals in all of the examples in this book. In Ex. 6-6, measure 8 in the alto, an F♮ is used because two F♯s had appeared a short time before. Without the natural sign, many altos will fall into the trap of singing another F♯.

Some cautionary accidentals are provided that cancel an accidental that has occurred in another voice or another octave. In Ex. 6-1, measure 12 in the left hand staff for the organ, an E♮ appears as a reminder since E♭ had appeared in the previous measure.

In versions since *Finale* 97, a plug-in called "Cautionary Accidentals" has been provided that will enter cancellation signs where needed. Some editions print parentheses around the cautionary accidentals. We discourage this practice because they clutter up the score and the extra space they take up tends to skew the representation of the rhythm. We do recommend, however, that in long measures with many notes, it is helpful to repeat an accidental near the end of the bar that appeared early in that bar, as shown in Ex. 6-10.

Ex. 6-10 Cautionary accidentals in long measures with many notes.

Getting help

You have many ways of getting help when needed. First, use the Online Documentation that comes with *Finale*. If you don't find the answer there, contact Coda Technical Support (612-937-9760). The *Finale* Productivity Tips site on the web at www.finaletips.nu includes a FAQ (frequently asked questions) section. There you will find a link to The *Finale* Discussion List where you can get immediate help from many knowledgeable users. Revisit the tutorials and watch the QuickStart Video Tips.

The author has written *Finale* tutorials which are available at: http://www.shsu.edu/%7Emus_heh/finale/

The file names are Tut2k.sit. (Mac) and tut2kpc.zip (Windows).

CHAPTER 7. Publication

The final draft of your creative project is finished and you are busy making a final copy, either by hand or with a computer. Any composition or arrangement is full of minute details that need to be checked and rechecked before copies are made for musicians, or it is prepared for submission to a publisher, or for publishing it yourself. If music or lyrics are used that are not in the public domain, you will need to secure permission for their use. You should have sought input from experienced composers and arrangers before this stage, but you should also get help from someone for proofreading as well.

Preparing Your Manuscript

Here are some frequently asked questions concerning preparation of manuscripts for publication.

1. *What paper size should I use for my final copy?*
2. *How many systems should I plan to have per page?*
3. *Is there a preferred order for entry of notation items?*
4. *How shall I go about proof-reading the final copy?*
5. *What information should I give concerning the original source of words or music that have been used in my work?*
6. *What do I need to do about words or music I am using that are under copyright (not in the public domain)?*
7. *Is it a good idea to get a reading or a performance of my work before sending it to a publisher? Should I send a recording? Is a synthesized performance acceptable?*

If final copy is prepared by hand, use manuscript paper that is designed for the format being used. Manuscript papers come in many shapes and formats, from octavo choral format to 10x12 in. score paper for large ensembles. The paper used should be of sufficient weight to handle the heavy ink you will be using for music notation (at least 24 lb.).

It is likely that the final score will be made with your computer, and 8.5x11 in. paper is what your printer takes. You will either design your own format or use a template that has been pre-formatted for the proper type of ensemble.

Determine from your sketch or earlier draft how many systems to allow per page and how many measures per system. Lay out the blank measures and repeat signs needed for the whole piece if possible before entering notes. It is helpful to enter notation items in several passes: notes, rests, ties, and articulations first, lyrics next, then slurs and phrase marks, dynamics, tempo markings and other text items, and finally title and subtitle, composer, arranger, writer, and translator information. If you are using a computer, do a final global spacing command and update the layout. Add word extensions for the lyrics when you know no more layout adjustments will be needed.

When your draft is completed, print out a copy or make a photocopy to use for proofreading. Make a copy for a competent musician friend to proof-read as well. As the creator of the work, you will tend to see what you want to see, not what's actually there. Your friend can find errors or omissions you may have missed.

Proofreading and final editing

You and your friend can use the checklist below for proofreading. Make bold colored marks to indicate places that need to be corrected or adjusted.

Spacing and alignment. Check carefully for crowding and collisions. Make sure that notes and lyrics are properly aligned.

Clefs, key signatures, time signatures. See that the proper clefs and key signatures are at the beginning of every line and that clef and key changes appear in the right places. Check key signatures for transposing instruments. Allow space in all parts for any clef change. Check that the time signature appears only at the beginning and at changes. When a new meter appears at the beginning of a system, make sure that it also appears on the staff after the previous bar line.

Complete measures. Check to see that all bars contain the correct total of time values. You may have left out rests or dots.

Ties, slurs, and phrase marks. Some ties may be missing or incomplete when they are at system breaks. Check for tie direction, especially in chords and when two parts are on a single staff. Check for slurs in melismas. Check phrase marks across system breaks.

Articulations. Adjust any articulation marks that are not centered above or below note heads, so that they are properly oriented when they appear next to beams.

Lyrics. Check for correct spelling, capitalization, and punctuation. Make sure the lyrics agree with your source. Check words of more than one syllable to see that hyphens are entered properly. Make sure there are word extensions for melismas on single and final syllables. If hyphens or word extensions continue on another system, make sure they are properly entered there.

Dynamics. See that you have given a beginning dynamic for all parts. Make sure you provide a dynamic marking after one or more bars of rest. Check to see that crescendos and diminuendos have a stated beginning and ending dynamic level. Check that dynamic markings for voices are placed above the staff and that they are entered below for instruments and between the staves for a grand staff.

Solo and tutti. Make sure that the score indicates when a vocal solo begins and when the section resumes singing.

Playing and singing instructions. Unless a whole piece is to be played "pizz.," be sure that "arco" appears when bowing is to resume. Similarly, check for beginning and ending of muted passages, stopped horn, *non vibrato*, and other effects. When 8va or 8vb are used, make sure that the score shows when these markings end.

Reviewers will notice any errors in notation, scoring, balance of parts, poor doubling, chord spacing, voice leading, note and word spelling, inappropriate use of instruments, ranges, tessitura, awkward keyboard writing, and all of the other elements we have discussed in earlier chapters. Your work may have artistic merit, but it might be rejected due to technical matters such as these. It is very unlikely that you would receive a response from a publisher saying "We like your piece very much, but if you would correct the poor doubling in measures p and q and the poor voice leading in measures x and y, we would reconsider it. In addition, it would be much easier to read if you had two systems on a page rather than four and used the standard clef for tenor, not the bass clef. The alignment is off in several places, and sometimes it's hard to read the lyrics when they are so crowded."

Credits and sources

When you are using preexisting music or text, name the composer, writer, or source and the best information you have on birth dates and death dates (as they apply), or year of composition or publication (for sources). For Biblical texts, state the book, chapter, and verse. For example, the Magnificat text is from Luke 1:46-55.

If your source for music or text is from the twentieth or twenty-first century, it is likely that the work is under copyright.

It is your responsibility to contact the copyright holder to get permission to use the work or a part of it. Be prepared to pay a fee for permission. You may be required to include in your score a copyright statement that the holder will give you. Library resources and the Internet can be helpful in locating copyright holders, or to determine if the work is in the public domain.

Trial run, performance, recording

Before you consider submitting your work to a publisher, you should have your musicians perform it, even if this is only a rehearsed read-through. Performance in a service or concert is better, and a good recording may be helpful to send along to a publisher. Synthesized or MIDI playback recordings are of dubious value to publishers, and some prefer not to receive them.

Sending Your Work to a Publisher

1. *How do I choose a publisher?*
2. *Should I send a cover letter along with the manuscript?*
3. *Should I send copies to several publishers at once?*
4. *If I have several works, should I send them all at once?*
5. *How do publishers respond? How long does it take for my work to be reviewed?*
6. *What does it mean if my work is not accepted?*

Most publishing houses serve a special group of customers, offering the kinds of music they will use and be willing to buy. Some publishers are devoted solely to church music. For others, church music is a division along with school music, large ensemble music, piano music, and teaching method books. One of the best ways to choose a publisher is to look through your library for works that most closely resemble your own and send to that publisher. Spend an hour at your local sheet music outlet store and browse through the sheet music, noting which publishers are most likely to be interested in your work. The person who does the ordering of sheet music can suggest likely publishers and provide you with addresses.

When you have selected a publisher, send a clear copy of your manuscript with a short (single page) cover letter describing your involvement in church music and a word or two about your musical background and training. Send only one or two pieces. If you have a collection of related pieces, one or two will suffice as examples. If they are accepted, you can then send the others. If your score calls for instruments other than a keyboard, send only the score, not the parts. If the publisher wants the parts, you can send them later.

It is not a good idea to send copies of your music to more than one publisher at a time. If your work is accepted by one of the publishers, you would probably want to stall until you heard from the others. If two accepted the work, you would have to withdraw your work from one of them, which is not good business practice.

The usual method for sending a manuscript is to put it in an envelope large enough so that the score does not have to be folded. A cardboard backing should be included so that the music will arrive undamaged. A few publishers will accept works submitted as e-mail attachments, but only after you have contacted them for permission. You will need to find out if they are equipped to read your computer files. This system works best for composers who have established a working relationship with a publisher.

In most cases, the publisher will send a card to tell you that your manuscript has been received. Reviewers normally have a backlog of manuscripts to review, so you should allow a reasonable amount of time to get a response. Six months is reasonable, but a year is not. You may get a response right away if your music does not suit the publisher's needs at the time. It may mean that your work falls outside of their targeted customer base. Or it may mean that their catalog already has works similar to the one you submitted.

Desktop Publishing

The quality of computer notation software and computer printers makes it possible for some church musicians to publish their own music. Desktop publishing is useful for music that is very specialized, or intended for a small group of users. If you are writing only for highly-trained professional performers, or if your church belongs to a very small denomination, you may be able to produce the limited quantity that will satisfy your target customers.

If publishing your work yourself, be prepared to promote, distribute, sell, and do the bookkeeping for your product. It may be possible for you to arrange with local dealers to stock your music, but you will have to settle with the dealers your commission on the sales.

Publishing your own music in a limited way may make it impossible at a later date to have an established company publish the same works since existing copies may be in violation of the company's copyright.

If you are the publisher, you will need to apply for copyright for your own works. While you are waiting for the copyright assignment, you can protect your work by sending yourself a copy by registered mail.

Royalty Contracts and Copyright

When your work has been accepted for publication, you will receive a Royalty Contract that states the terms by which you give the copyright to the publisher in return for royalties. The contract is sometimes called "Composer's Agreement," "Publishing Agreement," or "Assignment of Copyright." When you sign the contract, you agree to the terms stipulated in the contract. The contract is dated, your name and address are given as the composer (or writer), and the company's name appears as the publisher. The contract will state your royalty payment as a percentage of sales, usually 10%.

Most contracts include a statement that says the publisher will publish the work within a specified time (one or two years, usually). If the work is not published within this time limit, all rights to the work revert to you as the composer. If the publisher, after a stated amount of time, decides that the work will go "out of print," the copyright can be reassigned to you upon written request. Other terms that may be included are performance rights, inclusion of the work in an anthology, change of name, and notice that promotional copies will not earn royalties. The publisher usually sends you five to ten copies when the work is published.

As the composer, you testify that your work does not infringe upon any existing copyright. This is where you must prove that you have received permission from the copyright owner of any music or lyrics used in your work that are currently under copyright (see the section on "Credits and Sources" above). The permission may be granted if you pay a flat fee, but sometimes you must agree to share your royalties with the copyright owner of the source material.

If the lyrics for your work have been written by a friend and have not been copyrighted, you should arrange with the writer either to share the royalties or agree on a flat fee in exchange for permission to use the lyrics.

Final Proofs

Before publication, the publisher will send you proofs of your score for you to examine and edit if necessary. They will look wonderful to you, but you must proof-read them with the same care that you gave to the score before submitting it. Read through each part as if you were performing it, and indicate in the margin with a colored pen or pencil any errors made by the engraver. If you want to make changes or add markings that were not in your submitted copy, be prepared to pay for these changes. You may not agree with all aspects of style in these proofs, but they reflect the publisher's house style, and your Publishing Agreement includes your willingness to accept the publisher's house style.

APPENDIX A. Basic Principles of Contrapuntal Writing

Ex. A-1 demonstrates the principles of counterpoint summarized below.

Ex. A-1 O HEILAND, REISS with counterpoint above the *cantus firmus*.

In the example above, the numbers represent the harmonic intervals formed between the parts. Those encircled show dissonant intervals. Intervals larger than an octave are reduced to their simple equivalents (9 = 2, 10 = 3). Letters represent dissonant types. S = suspension, p = passing tone, n = neighbor tone, DN = double neighbor group, Camb = cambiata.

Definitions

Counterpoint and Polyphony

Counterpoint is the essence of polyphony. Contrapuntal music exhibits the following characteristics:

a. There are two or more distinguishable parts of roughly equal importance, sounding together.
b. Each part maintains a melodic identity.
c. The parts maintain independence both of rhythm and pitch.
d. They share metric and harmonic context.
e. They complement one another, creating a unified whole.
f. They often share motivic ideas.

Consonance and Dissonance

The concept of consonance and dissonance has changed through the centuries. During the common practice period (roughly between 1650 and 1900) the consonant intervals are the Perfect Prime, Perfect Fifth, Perfect Octave, Major and Minor Thirds and Sixths (and their octave equivalents—10ths, 12ths, 13ths, etc.). All other intervals are considered to be dissonant, including the Perfect Fourth and all augmented or diminished intervals. The dissonant intervals formed between the parts in Ex. A-1 are circled.

Today it is more convenient to think of intervals on a continuum from most stable (octave) to least stable (tritone). Although church music written today generally conforms to common practice period usage, styles closer to popular music and jazz treat sevenths and ninths a bit more freely.

The ratio of consonance to dissonance is about 3 or 4 to 1 in the Renaissance and Baroque. In the very chromatic music of the late nineteenth century, it changes to about 2 to 1. Only in atonal and serial music is there a chance that the ratio is reversed. In Ex. A-1 the ratio is 3 to 1.

Conjunct and Disjunct Melodic Motion

Conjunct or stepwise motion predominates over disjunct or leapwise motion. Consecutive leaps in one direction create the impression of a chord, usually a major or minor triad. Consecutive leaps that create a discord, such as D-G♯-C♯, should be avoided in tonal music. After a large leap, the melody proceeds by step in the opposite direction.

In Ex. A-1 conjunct motion exceeds disjunct motion in both parts.

Relative Motion of Parts

In two-part music, the following kinds of relative motion are found, arranged from most frequent to least frequent.

a. Oblique motion—one part moves while the other is stationary.
b. Contrary motion—the parts move in opposite directions.
c. Parallel motion—the parts move in the same direction, retaining the interval between them—almost always in thirds or sixths.
d. Similar motion—the parts move in the same direction, but the interval between them changes.

Parallel unisons, octaves, and fifths are avoided in contrapuntal music, although use of parallel fifths in counterpoint for more than two parts has been used by some composers since about 1920. Parallel motion involving dissonant intervals is a-voided as well. Parallel motion should not be confused, how-ever, with doubling. Two voices doubled in octaves are considered to be a single part. If sopranos and tenors are doubled in octaves in counterpoint with altos and basses doubled in octaves, there are only two contrapuntal parts.

There is oblique motion in every measure of Ex. A-1 except measures 5 and 16. Contrary motion appears in all but measures 1, 4, 9, and 10. Parallel motion occurs in measure 1 and twice in measures 5-6. Similar motion occurs in measure 6, 10, and 14.

Cadences

The ends of musical units—phrases, periods, sections, and the final ending—are marked by cadences. In Renaissance two-part cadences, the voices come to an octave or a unison by step in opposite direction. The interval sequence is 6 - 8 or 3 - 1. Tonal cadences often have SO to DO in the lower part, and TI to DO in the upper part. The upper part may proceed from RE to MI. In Ex. A-1, all the cadences have the interval sequence 6 to 8. They occur in measures 4, 8, 12, and 16 at the ends of the four phrases of the *cantus firmus.* These are *authentic cadences.*

Other types of cadences encountered in two-part counterpoint are the *half cadence,* which pauses on the dominant at the end of a phrase, the *plagal cadence* (subdominant to tonic), the *deceptive cadence* (dominant resolving to a harmony other than the tonic, promising an extension before a final cadence), and *modal cadences,* found in folk music and music of the Renaissance and Middle Ages.

Imitation and Canon

When the parts freely share musical ideas, we call it imitation. Canon is strict imitation that continues through a piece or section of a piece. The follower *(comes)* maintains a fixed distance in time and interval from the leader *(dux).* Canons at the unison or octave are most common, but canons at the fourth or fifth are frequently encountered. Canons at other intervals are rare, but Bach has given us examples in his *Goldberg Variations* and the *Canonic Variations on Vom Himmel Hoch.*

Mechanics of Species in Two-Part Counterpoint

Johann Fux devised a convenient system for the study of two-part counterpoint in his *Gradus ad Parnassum* (1725) that explained the use of consonances and dissonances in various rhythmic configurations. Fux's principles are summarized below. Measure numbers refer to Ex. A-1.

a. *First Species.* Note against note. When two parts move in the same rhythm, consonant intervals alone are used. Care should be taken that the interval sequences 1 - 1, 5 - 5, and 8 - 8 are avoided. First Species occurs in measures 1, 4, 5, 13 moving into the down beat of 14, and the final cadence.

b. *Second Species.* Two notes against one. The first note must make a consonance with the other part. The second note may make a consonance or a dissonance, provided it is a passing tone or neighbor tone. In measure 2, beat 3, the upper part has a passing tone. In bar 5, the B♭ is a neighbor tone. In bar 11, the G makes a consonant fifth with the lower part. The advent of the appoggiatura and the accented passing and neighbor tones in the early seventeenth century allows the first note to be a dissonance as long as the second is a consonance reached by step.

   c. *Third Species.* Three or more notes against one. The first note is consonant, but the others may be either consonant or dissonant as long as they are passing tones, neighbor tones, double neighbor groups (marked "DN" in the example) or form a cambiata (marked "Camb"). After about 1580, appoggiaturas, escape tones, accented passing and neighbor tones, and anticipations are admitted. Third Species examples appear in bars 2, 7, 8, 11, and 15.

   d. *Fourth Species.* The suspension. During the Renaissance, the suspension was the only dissonance permitted on strong beats. Suspensions consist of a preparation, suspension proper, and resolution. Each of these elements is carefully controlled, as shown in the table below.

Element	Metric position	Harmonic interval	Other requirements
Preparation	Relatively strong	Consonant	Equal to or longer than the suspension proper
Suspension proper	Relatively strong	Dissonant	Equal to or shorter than the preparation
Resolution	Strong or weak depending on the length of the suspension	Consonant, but not a unison or octave	Step below the suspension; it should be a different pitch from the note used against the suspension.

      In triple meter, the first or second beat can be the site of a suspension. In our example, suspensions occur in bars 3, 7, and 13, all on beat 2. Suspensions often occur just before a cadence to give it an added amount of tension. The note of preparation and suspension may be either tied across a bar line or a longer note that continues into the suspension proper. The tied notes between bars 1 and 2 and bars 10 and 11 are syncopations in rhythm, but since they do not create dissonances, they are not considered suspensions.

   e. *Fifth Species.* Use of first through fourth species in a single piece. Fux called this "florid counterpoint." Our example would be considered as Fifth Species.

Counterpoint in Three Parts

      The example below is a three-part setting of the chorale ERHALT UNS HERR. Examine the triads and seventh chords formed by the parts and the cadences at the ends of the phrases.

Ex. A-2 ERHALT UNS HERR in a three-part contrapuntal setting.

Intervals and dissonances are indicated as in Ex. A-1. The symbol "tt" represents the interval of a tritone. The letter "e" represents an escape tone (échappé), and the letters "ct" indicate the seventh used as a chord tone. Cadences are marked PAC for perfect authentic cadence, HC for half cadence, and IAC for imperfect authentic cadence.

In three-part counterpoint, there are three distinct sets of two-part counterpoint—bass and alto (the lower set of figures), bass and soprano (the upper set of figures), and alto and soprano (figures not given). All three sets conform to the principles of two-part counterpoint with the following exceptions:

a. Fourths and tritones may be used between alto and soprano when they combine with the bass to form triads. In the example, the fourths between soprano and alto in measure 4 create a minor triad in first inversion with the bass. In measure 7, the tritone between C and F♯ create a diminished triad in first inversion with the bass.
b. Parallel motion in two parts is often set against independent motion in the other part. The soprano and alto move in parallel sixths against the bass in measures 1-2. In measure 4, the alto and bass move in parallel tenths against the soprano.

The contrapuntal texture is maintained when:

a. each of the three parts has a different rhythm (see measure 3).
b. two of the parts move in the same rhythm against the third part (see measure 2).
c. all parts move in the same rhythm with some use of contrary motion (see measure 4, beat 3 to 4).

Triads are used freely in root position and first inversion. Second inversion triads are used only in cadential formulas or as the result of passing, neighboring, or arpeggio motion. Except when there is an arpeggio, the bass should move by step to a second inversion triad.

Cadences in three-part counterpoint are more fully defined by triadic progression. The perfect authentic cadence in measure 2 is V to i in G Minor. The half cadence in measure 4 is iv_6 - V. The imperfect cadence in measure 6 is V to I_6 in the relative major. The perfect authentic cadence in measure 8 is V^7 to i in G Minor.

The ratio of consonance to dissonance remains quite high. In our example it is about 5 to 1. All dissonant intervals are accounted for in the example by type of dissonance. If two parts move together creating dissonances with the third part, the two parts must make consonances with each other. An example of this is in measure 4 where alto and bass move in tenths to create dissonances with the soprano.

In Renaissance style, melodic leaps of a seventh, ninth, or any augmented or diminished interval are discouraged. In the Baroque period and afterwards, these leaps are permitted when they are part of a seventh chord. An example of this is the tritone leap in the alto, measure 7. Seventh chords in three-voice counterpoint usually omit the fifth, but the third may be o-mitted occasionally. Seventh chords may be used in any inversion provided they are properly resolved.

Three-part texture may be imitative, as in a fugue. The cantus firmus with accompanying counterpoint is a common texture, as in our example. Layered textures, such as Ex. 4-1c, are effective as well.

Counterpoint in Four or More Parts

The principles of three-part counterpoint apply as well to four or more parts, except that there is likely to be more parallel rhythm between any two parts. Spacing and doubling of chord members become important elements. The bass part begins to have a more harmonic role. These issues are taken up in Appendix B.

APPENDIX B. Basic Principles of Harmony and Part-Writing

This summary will help you recall the principles you learned as a student in harmony class.

Ex. B-1 "BROTHER JAMES' AIR" in a four-part setting.

Chord Analysis and Harmonic Function

The Roman Numeral System

Ex. B-1 shows a standard American roman numeral chord analysis. This system uses the following conventions.

a. Major triads are indicated in upper case, minor triads in lower case. Augmented triads are indicated in upper case with a plus sign (III$^+$), diminished triads in lower case with a small circle (vii°).

b. A roman numeral with no figures indicates root position. The figures $\frac{5}{3}$ are used to show when a chord moves from an inversion to root position.

c. Figures indicate the presence of sevenths (ninths, elevenths, thirteenths), and inversions. A ^{6} indicates a triad in first inversion. The figures $\frac{6}{4}$ indicate a triad in second inversion. Seventh chords in root, first, second, and third inversion are indicated with the figures ^{7}, $\frac{6}{5}$, $\frac{4}{3}$, and $\frac{4}{2}$.

d. Accidentals indicate alterations to diatonic chords.

e. The symbol °7 indicates a full diminished seventh chord; $\emptyset$ 7 indicates a half diminished seventh chord.

f. A sharp or flat in front of a roman numeral indicates the alteration of the root up or down a half step. For example, an E♭ Major triad in F Major is labeled ♭VII.

g. A series of figures, such as 4 – 3 indicates a suspension or appoggiatura and its resolution. An example appears in measure 4.

Primary, Secondary, and Modal Chords

a. The chords that define the key in major and minor are those built on the tonic, dominant, and subdominant. They are used in strong progressions and cadences. Note the strong progressions in measures 3-4 and 8-12.

b. The secondary chords are those built on the supertonic, mediant, and submediant. They provide harmonic variety and smoothness in harmonic progressions. Note the smooth progression in measures 2-3 and the harmonic variety in measures 5-7.

c. Leading-tone chords usually have a dominant function. The vii° should not be used in root position in music for more than three parts. The vii°7 and vii$^\emptyset$ 7 chords may be used in any position.

d. Modal alternative chords may be used in minor when scale degrees 6 or 7 are altered. They are the ii (RE-FA-LA), III+ (ME-SO-TI), IV (FA-LA-DO), and v (SO-TE-RE).

e. The tonic in minor may appear with the third raised (Picardy Third), and is indicated by the symbol I♯.

Harmonic Progression and Root Movement

a. The strongest harmonic progressions involve root movement by perfect fourth or fifth in either direction. Examples: IV–I into bar 1, V–I in bars 3–4 and 8–11, iii–vi in bar 5.

b. Root movement by third involves a change of harmonic color but is not as strong as movement by fourth or fifth. With diatonic chords whose roots are a third apart there will be two common tones. Examples: vi–I in bar 5 and IV–vi in bar 6.

c. Root movement by step produces smooth harmonic progressions and provides a feeling of forward motion. The progression from V to IV tends to sound weak (except when used in the context of "the blues").

d. A striking harmonic effect is achieved in chromatic music that involves chords whose roots are a third apart but have only one common tone or none at all. Equally striking is the progression from a dominant seventh chord to another whose root is a tritone away. These chords will have two common tones. Ex. 3-8 has several of these progressions.

Cadences

a. The authentic cadence, dominant to tonic, is the strongest and most common. The dominant chord becomes more "binding" when a seventh is added. The leading-tone chord can be used in place of the dominant (vii°6–I, or vii°7–i, for example).

b. The plagal cadence, subdominant to tonic, is nearly as strong as the authentic. Plagal cadences are marked in measures 8 and 12.

c. The half cadence is a pause on the dominant. It is often used at the end of the antecedent phrase in a period. The second phrase of OLD HUNDREDTH ends with a half cadence (see Ex. 4-3).

d. The deceptive cadence replaces the tonic chord in an authentic cadence with another chord, usually the submedient. The third phrase of OLD HUNDREDTH ends with a deceptive cadence (vii°6–vi).

e. Modal cadences emphasize the harmonic character of the mode. Dorian: IV–i, Phrygian: vii°⁶–i, Lydian: II-I, Mixolydian: v⁷–I, and Aeolian: v-i are examples.

f. A cadence is called "perfect" if the final chord has the root as its highest and lowest notes. Any other chord setting is called "imperfect." All of the cadences in Ex. 2-7 are imperfect except the last.

g. A regional cadence is an authentic cadence to a key other than the tonic. In Ex. 1-2 there is a regional cadence to the dominant in measure 8 and a regional cadence to the subdominant in measure 12.

Principles of Part-Writing

The principles given here have guided composers of tonal music throughout the "common practice period" (roughly from 1650-1900 and traditional music written since then, including most church music). They should be considered as guidelines rather than strict rules.

Voice Leading

a. Chord members generally move by step to the next chord with the exception that the bass part may have leaps, especially at cadences.

b. Common tones are usually retained in the same voice.

c. Active tones of the scale move by step in most cases (RE-DO, TI-DO, FA-MI or ME, LA or LE-SO).

d. Tones that have been raised by half step resolve up. Tones lowered by half step resolve down. In the melodic form of the minor upward movement from SO involves LA and TI on the way to DO. Downward motion involves TE and LE on the way to SO.

e. Parallel motion involves thirds, sixths, or tenths most of the time. Parallel fourths may occur in inner voice movement. Parallel unisons, seconds, fifths, sevenths, and octaves are discouraged.

f. Similar or parallel motion of all parts is avoided except for motion within the same harmony or in *fauxbourdon*— parallel first inversion chords.

g. Soprano and bass parts should move in oblique or contrary motion as much as possible. Parallel motion between the outer voices tends to move the whole ensemble up and down in waves and the music tends to lack variety of voicings.

h. Tones comprising the interval of a tritone resolve by step in contrary motion. The °5 contracts; the +4 expands.

i. Dissonances are usually approached and left by step with the exception of the double-neighbor group, the escape tone, and the appoggiatura which can be approached by leap.

j. Leaps of augmented or diminished intervals should be avoided unless the tones involved are members of the current harmony.

k. In music with five or more parts, motion within a chord can be used to avoid parallel unisons, fifths, or octaves.

Doubling

a. The roots of chords are most often doubled.

b. The third may be doubled in minor triads or when the voices approach it in contrary motion. Examples: the ii and IV chords in bar 2, the vi chord in bar 5, the IV chord in bar 6 and the I chord in bar 11.

c. The leading tone should not be doubled, nor should altered tones acting as leading tones in secondary dominant chords and in regional cadences.

d. Chord sevenths, ninths, elevenths, or thirteenths should not be doubled.

e. The fifth may be doubled or omitted in triads or seventh chords. The third is omitted in an eleventh chord, and the fifth is omitted in a thirteenth chord.

f. The third is normally doubled in the vi chord in a deceptive cadence, in the Neapolitan sixth chord, and in the Italian augmented sixth chord.

g. In music with more than four parts, any chord member may be doubled. The root is doubled most and occasionally trebled.

Chord Voicing

a. Both close and open voicing are appropriate for three-part music. The inner voice may at times be close to the top voice or to the bottom voice, and the interval between it and either of the other voices may occasionally exceed an octave. Voicing that results in more than an octave between the middle voice and both outer voices, however, should be avoided.

b. In four-part music, the distance between alto and soprano and between tenor and alto should not exceed an octave. This restriction does not apply to the distance from the bass to the tenor.

c. Close voicing in low registers tends to sound muddy and should be avoided.

d. Open voicing in choral music is best for louder passages; close voicing is best for softer passages.

Inversions

a. Root position harmonies are stable and most suitable for establishing the key and for strong cadences. First inversion triads provide variety and a sense of motion to progressions. Second inversion triads are unstable, and their use is restricted. Ex. B-2 shows several ways that the triad in $\frac{6}{4}$ position can be used.

Ex. B-2 Second inversion triads in "Aurelia".

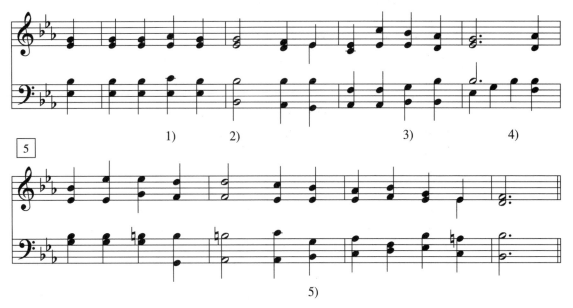

1) Neighbor $\frac{6}{4}$
2) Appoggiatura $\frac{6}{4}$
3) Cadential $\frac{6}{4}$
4) Arpeggio $\frac{6}{4}$
5) Passing $\frac{6}{4}$

b. The bass may approach the cadential, arpeggio, and appoggiatura $\frac{6}{4}$ chords by step or leap. The neighbor and passing $\frac{6}{4}$ chords should be approached by step in the bass.

APPENDIX C. Chord Symbols

Two widely-used systems for identification of individual harmonies and chords have been used in this book. The first is found in song books and "lead sheets" to show chords appropriate for accompaniment by guitar or keyboard. The other is the traditional Roman Numeral System used for chord analysis.

Lead Sheet Chord Symbols

1. The initial letter indicates the root of the chord.

2. If the initial letter appears alone or with an accidental, the chord is assumed to be a major triad. In some systems, a lower case letter indicates a minor triad.
   Examples: A = A-C♯-E, E♭ = E♭-G-B♭, d = D-F-A.

3. Letters or special symbols after the initial letter indicate chord quality. "M" or "Maj" indicates major, "m" or "min" indicates minor. Diminished triads are indicated by "dim" or the symbol "○". Examples: Gm = G-B♭-D, B○ = B-D-F.

4. Numbers indicate notes added to the basic triad. A7 is assumed to be a minor seventh unless otherwise indicated. A9 designates a diatonic ninth, unless an alteration symbol is given, and assumes the presence of a minor seventh as well. Examples: F6 = F-A-C-D, G7 = G-B-D-F, D9 = D-F♯-A-C-E, C♭9 = C-E-G-B♭-D♭.

5. The expression "sus4" indicates a triad with a fourth above the root instead of the third. For example: Csus4 = C-F-G.

6. Extended chords such as 11th and 13th chords usually assume a minor 7th and diatonic 9th is to be included unless otherwise indicated. Example: D13 = D-F♯-C-E-B

7. Symbols in parentheses indicate chord members added or altered, a ♭ lowers the tone a half step, a ♯ raises it a half step. Example: Bm7(♭5) = B-D-F-A. This chord may also be indicated as B∅ (a B half-diminished seventh chord) .

8. A letter following a slash indicates the bass note when it is not the root of the chord. Examples: F/A = A-C-F (F major with A in the bass), G/C = C-G-B-D (G major played above a C in the bass).

9. Some systems use the minus sign (–) to indicate minor triads. This practice is not recommended because of the confusion that can occur with other uses of that symbol. The plus sign (+) indicates an augmented triad.

Roman Numeral Chord Symbols

1. The *chord root* is indicated by a Roman numeral that corresponds to the scale degree upon which the chord is built. For example, a D major triad in the key of A major is the IV chord.

2. The *case* of the Roman numeral, with the possible inclusion of other symbols, indicates the chord's triadic quality. Upper case indicates major triad quality. Lower case indicates minor triad quality. If a + is added, an augmented triad quality is indicated. If a ° is added, a diminished triad quality is indicated.

3. If no figures appear next to the Roman numeral, root position is assumed. The figures $\frac{5}{3}$ may be used to show when a chord has moved from an inversion to root position.

4. Figures indicate the presence of sevenths (and ninth, eleventh, or thirteenth chords in root position) and inversions of triads and seventh chords. The figures always represent interval distance measured above the bass. Intervals in triads are indicated in close position (10th = 3d, 12th = 5th, etc.).

5. Accidentals indicate alterations to diatonic chords. The symbol I♯ indicates raised third in a tonic chord that is normally minor, the "Picardy third."

6. The diminished and augmented signs (+ and °) next to a number indicate specific chords. The symbol +6 indicates an augmented sixth chord, the symbol °7 indicates a (full) diminished seventh chord, and the symbol ø7 indicates a half-diminished seventh chord.

7. A sharp or flat in front of a Roman numeral shows alteration of the root up or down a half step. For example, ♭VII indicates a

lowered leading tone chord. In the key of D minor, ♭VII is a C major triad.

The chart below shows Roman numerals for triads built on each degree of the major and minor scales.

QUALITY OF DIATONIC TRIADS

Root Scale Degree	Scale Degree Name	Triad Quality in Major Keys	Symbol	Triad Quality in Minor Keys	Symbol	Modal Alternates
1	Tonic	Major	I	Minor	i	I♯(Picardy 3rd)
2	Supertonic	Minor	ii	Diminished	ii°	ii
3	Mediant	Minor	iii	Major	III	III⁺
4	Subdominant	Major	IV	Minor	iv	IV
5	Dominant	Major	V	Major	V	v
6	Submediant	Minor	vi	Major	VI	
7	Leading-tone	Diminished	vii°	Diminished	vii°	♭VII (V of III)

Ex. D-1 Hymn tune SONG 46 by Orlando Gibbons showing Lead Sheet and Roman Numeral Chord Symbols.

APPENDIX D. Instrument Ranges

For each instrument, the filled notes show lowest and highest possible pitches; the open notes show practical ranges for church music applications.

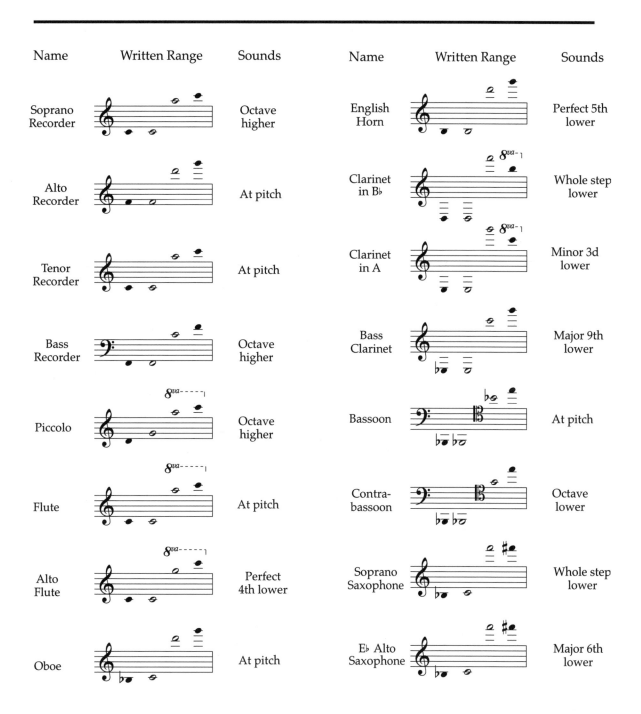

Name	Written Range	Sounds	Name	Written Range	Sounds
Soprano Recorder		Octave higher	English Horn		Perfect 5th lower
Alto Recorder		At pitch	Clarinet in B♭		Whole step lower
Tenor Recorder		At pitch	Clarinet in A		Minor 3d lower
Bass Recorder		Octave higher	Bass Clarinet		Major 9th lower
Piccolo		Octave higher	Bassoon		At pitch
Flute		At pitch	Contra-bassoon		Octave lower
Alto Flute		Perfect 4th lower	Soprano Saxophone		Whole step lower
Oboe		At pitch	E♭ Alto Saxophone		Major 6th lower

Name	Written Range	Sounds	Name	Written Range	Sounds

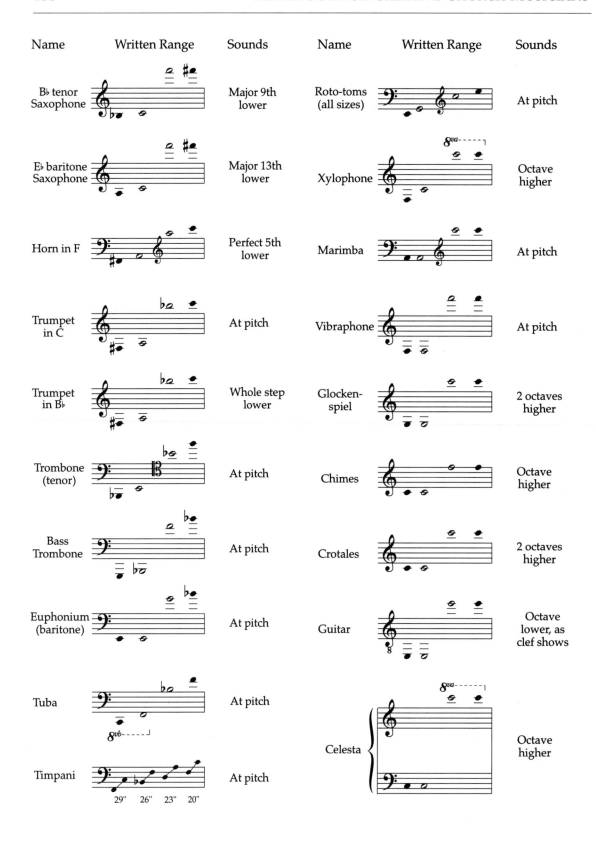

Name	Written Range	Sounds	Name	Written Range	Sounds

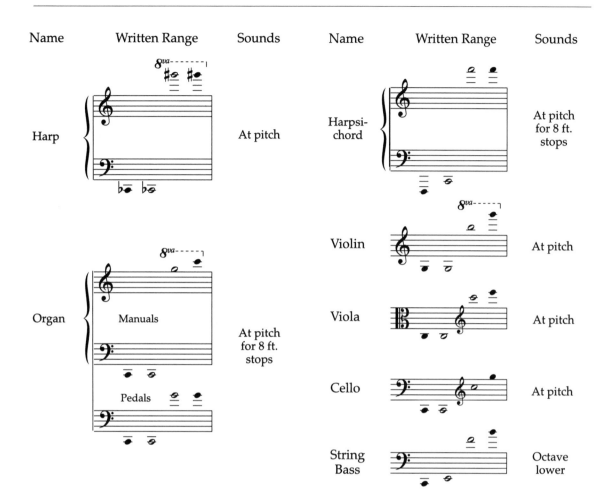

Notes on the instrument ranges

The upper limits of pitch for woodwind and brass instruments can be extended somewhat by extraordinary performers. Some very skilled hornists and trombonists can play somewhat lower than indicated above. The upper limit of the stringed instruments can be extended to include harmonics.

Bass clarinet is sometimes written in bass clef in concert pitch so that it can substitute for bassoon. In very old scores, low horn parts using bass clef sounded a Perfect 4th above the written notes. Today, however, the sounding pitches are a Perfect 5th below in both treble and bass clef.

Some models of flute can play down to B. Some bass clarinets have an extension that takes the range down to D, sounding pitch of Low C. Some contra bassoons have a low A. Parts for euphonium (baritone) are written in treble clef, in which case the sounding pitches are a Major 9th lower. Timpani also come in a 32" model with a compass of Low D to the A a fifth higher.

Some marimbas extend the range down to E or even to low C, but these are rare. The lowest note on most marimbas is A, as shown in the chart.

The ranges given for organ and harpsichord reflect the 8 ft. pipes or strings that sound at pitch. The lower octave is available with 16 ft. stops. The upper octave is available with 4 ft. stops, which sound an octave higher than notated. The 32 ft pipes sound two octaves lower, and 2-ft. pipes and strings sound two octaves higher.

String bass instruments in most larger orchestras have either an extension allowing the E string to be lowered by half steps down to C or a fifth string, tuned to C below Low C.

We have included instruments you are most likely to use. Information concerning instruments less frequently encountered, such as the bass flute, oboe d'amore, basset-horn, flügelhorn, mandolin, and viols can be found in orchestration books and music encyclopedias.

LIST OF HYMN TUNES AND OTHER MUSICAL EXAMPLES

This list includes complete examples and excerpts of hymn tunes, anthems, chants, and organ works used in this book. Common names of some hymn tunes are included.

GLOSSARY

A cappella. Choral music without instrumental accompaniment.

Accent. A marking on a note or chord indicating that it is to be given emphasis in performance.

Anticipation. A non-harmonic tone that is sounded before it becomes a part of the harmony when repeated.

Appoggiatura. A tone that makes a dissonance with the chord with which it is sounded. It is most often approached by a leap of a third or more, and it resolves down by step to a chord member before the harmony changes.

Atonal. Music in which no tonic or tonal center is established.

Augmented interval. An interval that has been increased in size by a half step. Example: F to G is a Major second. F to G♯ is an Augmented second.

Augmented triad. A triad consisting of two Major thirds stacked vertically, such as C-E-G♯. The interval from C to G♯ is an Augmented fifth.

Auxiliary tone. See *neighbor tone*.

Basic pitches. Tones of structural importance in a melody.

Blue notes. Notes traditionally lowered in blues style melody, usually the third and seventh degrees of the major scale.

Borrowed chords. Chords are "borrowed" from a parallel mode to replace diatonic chords. Examples: A major subdominant used in the minor mode; a minor dominant used in the major mode.

Cambiata. *Nota cambiata* or changing note, a three or four note figure used mainly in fifteenth and early sixteenth century polyphony consisting of a step down, leap of a third down, step up. The second note of the group is dissonant with other parts.

Canon. Strict imitation of one part by one or more other parts sustained throughout a work or a section of a work. Imitation may be at the unison, octave, or other interval (most often perfect fourth or fifth), and the distance in time between leader and follower(s) remains fixed (a beat, a half measure, a measure, multiple measures, etc.)

Cantus firmus. A pre-existing melody, often presented in long note values, to which counterpoint may be added. Chant and chorale melodies are the most commonly used.

Chorale. The congregational song or hymn of the German Protestant Church. It referred originally to a hymn text, but by the seventeenth century, it referred to a hymn tune and associated text. Since the eighteenth century, it has come to refer to a four part setting of a hymn tune with associated text. For example, "Ein feste Burg" may refer to Martin Luther's original tune and text or to J. S. Bach's settings of the tune.

Chord root. The lowest tone of a chord when it is given in root position.

Church modes. Scale structures other than major and minor used during the Middle ages and Renaissance, in much of Western folk music, and in the twentieth century. Also called *ecclesiastical modes*, their names have been borrowed from the Greek modal system: Dorian, Phrygian, Lydian, Mixolydian, and Aeolian.

Close voicing. Harmonies arranged with the chord members close together.

Conjunct. Melodic motion by step.

Contrapuntal. Musical texture involving two or more melodic lines with independent melodic and rhythmic motion.

Contrary motion. Pitch movement of two parts in opposite direction.

Counterpoint. (1) Music in which there are two or more distinguishable parts, each maintaining independence of the others in pitch and rhythmic movement. The parts complement one another, usually sharing metric and harmonic context. They also often share motivic ideas. (2) The study of polyphonic music through analysis and composition. (3) A part or group of parts set to a given melody.

Cross-relation. The dissonance caused by the close proximity in two different voices of a diatonic pitch and an altered form of that pitch. Example: E♮ and E♭.

Cross rhythm. Rhythmic motion that goes against the prevailing meter.

Descant. A decorative counterpoint added to a given melody such as a hymn tune.

Diminished interval. An interval that has been decreased in size by a half step. Example: C to G is a Perfect Fifth. C to G♭ is a Diminished Fifth.

Diminished triad. A triad consisting of two Minor thirds stacked vertically, such as C-E♭-G♭. The interval from C to G♭ is a Diminished fifth.

Disjunct. Melodic motion by leap of a third or more.

Dominant. In music theory, the fifth degree of the scale and the harmony built upon it.

Double neighbor. A four note melodic figure in which the second note is the upper neighbor and the third note is the lower neighbor to the first and fourth. The lower neighbor may come before the upper neighbor as well.

Dynamics. Markings in a score that indicate fixed or changing degrees of loudness or softness.

Échappée. See *escape tone.*

Escape tone. A non-harmonic tone that is the second note in a three note melodic figure consisting of a step up and a third down. Example: D-E-C, where E is non-harmonic. Also called *échappée.*

Fermata. Marking in a score indicating that notes or rests are to be held beyond their normal time value.

Full cadence. The ending of a musical phrase, period, or section that gives a feeling of conclusiveness. Example: V to I progression.

Half cadence. The ending of a musical phrase or section that gives a feeling of inconclusiveness. Example: IV to V progression.

Harmonic rhythm. The rate of harmonic change, usually expressed in the number of harmonic changes per measure.

Harmonic series. The fundamental (frequency f) and all overtones (2f, 3f, 4f, 5f, 6f, etc.) present in a complex tone. All members of the harmonic series are called *partials.*

Harmonics. Tones in the harmonic series other than the fundamental. Synonymous with *overtones.*

Harmony. (1) The effect produced by tones sounding together. (2) Chordal progression. (3) The study of homophonic music through analysis and composition.

Hemiola. A musical gesture wherein a rhythmic figure with a duple metric pulse alternates with one with a triple metric pulse.

Homophony. Melody with subordinate accompanying parts.

Homorhythmic. Music in which the parts move in the same rhythm.

Inversion (harmonic). A chord whose root is not the lowest sounding tone. A first inversion chord has its third as the lowest tone. A second inversion chord has the fifth as its lowest tone. A seventh chord in third inversion has the seventh as its lowest tone.

Inversion (melodic). A melodic line that is turned upside down, rendering each melodic interval in the opposite direction.

Key. The prevailing mode and its tonic pitch name. Examples: D Major, A Minor, C Dorian. A musical passage may or may not bear the signature associated with the prevailing key.

Lead sheet. A term used in jazz and popular music for the notation of a melody with chord symbols.

Leading tone. The seventh degree of the major and harmonic minor scales.

Melisma. Two or more tones sung to a single syllable.

Melismatic. Music in which the number of notes is noticeably greater than the number of syllables of text.

Meter. The organization of the beat or tactus into regularly recurring patterns of stresses and unstresses, also called the *time signature*.

MIDI. Musical Instrument Digital Interface. A digital protocol that specifies pitch, velocity, and other tonal aspects recognized by synthesizers, computer music programs, and other digital musical devices.

Modal. Music created from scales other than the major and minor.

Mode. (1) In general, any diatonic scale, including major and minor (2) One of the church modes, Dorian, Phrygian, Lydian, Mixolydian, Aeolian.

Modulation. The process of changing from one key or mode to another.

Monophony. Unaccompanied melody.

Motive. The smallest unit of music that has enough character to be subsequently developed.

Neighbor tone. A tone that is a step above or below the pitch that precedes and follows it. It is also called *auxiliary tone*.

Non-harmonic tones. Decorative pitches that are not members of the harmony that accompanies them. Also called *complementary tones*.

Oblique motion. Part-writing in which one part moves while another part is stationary.

Open score. A musical score where each part is given its own staff.

Open voicing. Harmonies arranged with the chord members spread apart.

Ostinato. A repeating figure, often in the bass, but can be used in any part.

Overtones. Harmonics or partials above the fundamental pitch of a complex tone. The relative strength of the overtones contributes to the perception of tone quality.

Parallel motion. Two or more parts move in the same direction maintaining the interval size between them. Interval quality may or may not remain constant. Examples: Parts on C and G move respectively to D and A, creating a set of parallel fifths (both perfect); Parts on G and B move to D and F, creating a set of parallel thirds (one major and the other minor).

Part-writing. The movement of each part or voice in relationship with the others and the role of each part in the creation of harmony.

Passing tone. A non-harmonic pitch that connects by step two harmonic pitches a third apart. Example: C-D-E, where C and E are harmonic and D is the passing tone. Two passing tones may occur next to each other. Example: E-F♯-G♯-A or C-B♮-B♭-A.

Pedal point. Originally a tone sustained in the organ pedals while music on the manuals moves above it. The term is now used to describe any sustained or repeated tone, most often in the bass but occasionally in other registers, against which the other parts move.

Period. Two or more phrases that form a cohesive unit, with the last phrase ending in a more conclusive cadence than any that precede it.

Phrase. A relatively complete musical idea ending with some kind of cadence.

Picardy Third. Alteration of the third of a tonic minor chord changing its quality to major. It often appears as the final chord in a piece or section in the minor mode.

Polyphony. Music for two or more voices in a contrapuntal texture.

Quartal harmony. In the strict sense, harmony based on the interval of the perfect fourth, rather than the third, as in tertian harmony; in a broader sense, music in which the perfect fourth, major second, and minor seventh are treated like consonances (as well as the perfect unison, octave, and fifth, and the major and minor thirds and sixths).

Regional progression. A succession of harmonies that temporarily establishes a key that is closely related to the original key.

Register. The relative pitch location (high, medium, low) for the particular instruments or voices being considered.

Root. See *chord root*.

Root position. A chord arranged so that its root is the lowest tone.

Secondal harmony. Music in which chordal structures emphasize major and minor seconds.

Secondary dominant chords. Chords with a dominant relationship to diatonic triads other than the tonic. Also called *applied dominant chords.*

Sequence. The repetition of a musical idea at one or more different pitch levels.

Staccato. A type of articulation where a note is played or sung very short—for only a fraction of its given time value. It is indicated in the score by a dot placed above or below the note-head.

Suspension. A tone that becomes dissonant when suspended over a change of harmony, then resolves downward to make a consonance.

Syncopation. A rhythmic figure where notes are sounded on weak beats and sustained through strong beats.

Tertian harmony. Harmony based on thirds, or triadic harmony, the basis of the tonal system of the common practice period.

Tessitura. The predominant register where a vocal (or instrumental) part lies.

Through-composed. A composition that develops from beginning to end without repetitions. The term is also used to denote a song in which each verse is set to different music.

Tonal. (1) Adhering to the system of major and minor as distinct from modal and atonal. (2) Exhibiting a hierarchy of tones in which certain tones assume the role of tonic, especially at cadence points.

Tonal center. The tone that is perceived as the principal one to which other tones are related.

Tonality. The organized relationship of pitches in which one functions as the center or tonic.

Tonic. The first degree of any scale or mode.

Triad. A chord consisting of three pitches: the root or basic pitch, the third (a third above the root), and the fifth (a fifth above the root). See also *inversion (harmonic), root position.*

Trill. A musical ornament consisting of the rapid alternation of one tone with another that is a whole step or half step above it.

Tuplet. Any grouping of notes that goes against the expected division or subdivision of the meter or the beat. Most common is the triplet that has three notes in the space of two.

Voice-leading. See *part-writing.*

SELECTED BIBLIOGRAPHY

Counterpoint

BENJAMIN, THOMAS. *The Craft of Modal Counterpoint: A Practical Approach.* New York: Schirmer Books, 1979.

_____. *Counterpoint in the Style of J. S. Bach.* New York: Schirmer Books, 1986.

GAULDIN, ROBERT. *A Practical Approach to Sixteenth-Century Counterpoint.* Englewood Cliffs, New Jersey: Prentice-Hall, Inc., 1984.

_____. *A Practical Approach to Eighteenth-Century Counterpoint.* Englewood Cliffs, New Jersey: Prentice-Hall, Inc., 1988.

KENNAN, KENT. *Counterpoint, Based on Eighteenth-Century Practice.* 3rd ed. Englewood Cliffs, New Jersey: Prentice-Hall, Inc., 1987.

OWEN, HAROLD. *Modal and Tonal Counterpoint, Josquin to Stravinsky.* New York: Schirmer Books, 1992.

SCHUBERT, PETER. *Modal Counterpoint, Renaissance Style,* New York: Oxford University Press, 1999.

SMITH, CHARLOTTE. *A Manual of Sixteenth-Century Contrapuntal Style.* Newark: University of Delaware Press, 1989.

Harmony and Theory

BENJAMIN, THOMAS, HORVITT, NELSON. *Techniques and Materials of Tonal Music.* 5th ed. New York: Schirmer Books, 1998

KOSTKA, STEFAN AND PAYNE, DOROTHY. *Tonal Harmony.* New York: McGraw-Hill, Inc., 1996.

KRAFT, LEO. *Gradus*: *An integrated approach to harmony, counterpoint, and analysis.* New York: W.W. Norton, 1976.

PISTON, WALTER, DE VOTO, MARK. *Harmony.* 4th ed. New York: W. W. Norton, 1978

OWEN, HAROLD. *Music Theory Resource Book.* New York: Oxford University Press. 2000

OTTMAN, ROBERT. *Advanced Harmony, Theory and Prectice.* Englewood Cliffs, New Jersey: Prentice Hall, 1984.

SPENCER, PETER. *The Practice of Harmony.* 4th ed. Upper Saddle River, New Jersey: Prentice Hall, 2000.

Choral Arranging, Orchestration, and Publication

ADLER, SAMUEL. *The Study of Orechestration.* New York: W. W. Norton, 1982

BLATTER, ALFRED. *Instrumentation and Orchestration.* New York: Schirmer Books, 1997.

HARLOW, BARBARA. *How to Get Your Choral Composition Published.* Santa Barbara, California: Santa Barbara Music Publishing. 1998.

HINES, ROBERT S. *Choral Composition.* New York: Oxford University Press. In preparation.

KENNAN, KENT. *The Technique of Orchestration.* 3d ed. New York: Prentice Hall, 1983

OSTRANDER, ARTHUR AND WILSON, DANA. *Contemporary Choral Arranging.* Englewood Cliffs, New Jersey.\: Prentice Hall, 1986.

Music Notation

HEUSSENSTAMM, GEORGE. *The Norton Manual of Music Notation.* New York: W. W. Norton, 1987

PURSE, BILL. *The Finale Primer: Mastering the Art of Music Notation with Finale.* Miller Freeman, Inc., Book Division, 2000

READ, GARDNER. *Music Notation: A Manual of Modern Practice.* 2nd ed. Taplinger Publishing Co., 1995

ROSS, TED. *The Art of Musical Engraving and Processing.* Miami: Hansen Books, 1970.

STONE, KURT. *Music Notation in the Twentieth Century: A Practical Guidebook.* New York: W. W. Norton, 1980

INDEX